A Children's Treasury of
FOLK AND
FAIRY TALES

A Children's Treasury of
FOLK AND
FAIRY TALES

Edited and adapted by ERIC PROTTER

Introduction by MARTHA FOLEY

*Illustrations by Bertall, Wilhelm Busch, Gustave Doré,
Heinrich Hoffman, Hildegard Hostnig, E. Mazzanti, Karl Merkel,
Willy Planck, Ludwig Richter, and Willy Widmann*

BEAUFORT BOOKS, INC.

New York/Toronto

This book is for
LISA

Library of Congress Cataloging in Publication Data
Main entry under title:

A Children's treasury of folk and fairy tales.

    Summary: A selection of traditional tales from Russia, Germany, Greece, France, Sweden, and other countries.
    1. Tales. [1. Folklore. 2. Fairy tales]
I. Protter, Eric.
PZ8.1.C435 1982   398.2'1   83–4387
ISBN 0–8253–0112–2   AACR2

Printed in the United States of America by Beaufort Books, Inc., New York. Published simultaneously in Canada by General Publishing Co. Limited

Printed in the U.S.A.   First Edition

10 9 8 7 6 5 4 3 2 1

ACKNOWLEDGMENTS

I acknowledge with deep gratitude the assistance given in translations by Salvator Attanasio, Bernard Frechtman, Nora McGrath, Nancy Protter, Elizabeth Williams, and Harriet Anderson.

Grateful acknowledgment for dedicated assistance must go to the staffs of the Bibliothéque Nationale, Paris; the library of the British Museum; and the New York Public Library.

The illustrations by Willy Planck are taken from "Rübezahl, Sagen und Schwänke," published by Loewes Verlag Ferdinand Carl, Stuttgart, Germany, and are reprinted by permission. These drawings appear on pages 146, 150, 153 and 156.

The illustrations by Hildegard Hostnig are taken from "Alpensagen" and "Volkssagen aus Aller Welt," published by Julius Breitschopf Jun., Vienna, Austria, and are used by permission. These drawings appear on pages 2, 42, 59, 60, 86, 94, 178, 182 and 188.

The illustrations by Willy Widmann are taken from "Sagen der Verlorenen Heimat," published by Carl Ueberreuter, Vienna, Austria, and are used by permission. These drawings appear on pages 100, 104, 108, 116, 122, 124, 126, 128, 134 and 137.

Adrian Ludwig Richter, whose illustrations appear throughout the book (pages 4, 7, 10, 15, 21, 23, 33, 35, 82, 88, 114, 131, 195, 198, 200, 204 and 212), was a German painter and one of the great illustrators of his time. Born in 1803, he died in 1884.

The gay little drawings by Wilhelm Busch, illustrating "Plish and Plum" (pages 161–164) and the Max and Moritz poems (pages 168–175), are typical of the work of this German artist, satirist, and writer of humorous verse. He was born in 1832 and died in 1908.

Dr. Heinrich Hoffman (1804–1894), a German best known for his "Der Struwwelpeter," is represented by "Flying Robert" (page 165) and "Johnny Head-in-Air" (pages 166–167), in the latter of which one of his own illustrations is reproduced.

Single illustrations by Karl Merkel (1817–1897), Bertall (1820–1883), E. Mazzanti (the original illustrator of "Pinocchio"), and Gustave Doré appear on pages 47, 79, 41 and 74, respectively.

—Eric Protter

Preface

When my publisher asked me to write a preface for this new edition of *A Children's Treasury of Folk and Fairy Tales,* I felt at a loss. What could I possibly add to the understanding introduction written by Martha Foley? So, I have decided to use this space to thank her, at least in spirit, for this fine woman left us a few years ago. Always the optimist (despite great tragedies in her life), she looked to the good in human beings rather than the base. She fought for what she believed was right and moral, even against great odds. And, like the heroine of many classic fairy tales, she was to be found on the side of the underdog. She questioned continuously our morality; she abhorred selfishness and greed. For instance, she could not understand why people took so little time to treat each other with honesty and concern. She never accepted the drive for wealth, success, and fame if it had to be accomplished at someone's expense.

Her modesty, intelligence and caring for life are legend, and they reflect her enduring spirit in the memory of those who knew her.

In this revised edition I have deleted three stories and have added three new ones. Two of those cut were for the very young and seemed somewhat out of place now. The third was a great story, the legend of William Tell, but it belongs more appropriately in a collection of legends rather than fairy tales.

The new stories have their roots in Ireland, Andorra, and Brittany. They are Celtic tales and so reflect their own special environment and culture.

E. P.
(May, 1982)

Introduction

"Tell me a story!" In all languages, in all countries, children of all races, from time before time was even measured, have made this plea. Long before there were books, stories were told to children. The tales they were told grew up with these children, and, as they migrated to new lands, the tales traveled with them, becoming a world-wide currency of culture. Thus it is that ancient stories of the Orient found their way into the countries of Europe even more surely than the spices and jewels of the East. In Europe they were adapted and blended with that Continent's own native stories for a thousand years and more. And from Europe they are brought to America in this fine collection by Eric Protter.

These are time-tested stories that have lasted because of a deep vitality in them. I sometimes think that, just as the human embryo passes through all the physical stages through which the human race has evolved, so do our minds and emotions. The primitive mind of the primitive man is still sleeping within us—sometimes not sleeping as much as it should!—and the gropings toward understanding by the peasant, the magician, the prince of earlier times are still all a part of what we think and feel.

Sometimes it is hard for people who have not worked in literary fields—sometimes even for those who have done such work, but do not grasp what depths can lie behind the face of simplicity—to understand that all our stories and folk tales grew out of something real, something that once happened and was important. This is why we have the old stories: because those events were considered important enough to be passed on from generation to generation, so that they would not be forgotten. Perhaps I should say the *people* in the stories were important because what they had learned from the events that had happened to them could be used to instruct as well as to entertain younger members of a new generation. Stories, after all, are not only made by people—they are about people. The stories have changed, of course, in their travels and on the lips of the varying kinds of people who have passed them on to us. They have been changed with telling, but the core of truth is still there.

Children, just as the human race once was, are still close to the magical. Their eyes behold wonders in the life beginning to stretch before them. Who can blame them? They love witches and fairies, good or bad, and magicians. Animals fascinate them. It is a rare child who does not love animals and want to be kind to them. Those of us who live in cities forget, if we ever once lived in the country, how close we felt as children to the animals around us. Children, so often awed and ordered around by adults, also can identify with the peasant who gets the better of a man who considers himself shrewd and important. Kindness, humility, courage, perseverance, hard work and not damning people because of an unprepossessing exterior are rewarded in these stories.

So these old tales are not so very old after all. They stay forever young because the people in them do the same things people do today. The same things happen to them. Only their titles are different. Instead of being Supreme Court Justices and Senators and Cabinet members, in these stories they are kings and princes and sultans. Instead of being dressed in old, wet clothes, they may be bears and frogs who are really important persons in disguise. It is much more fun for children to think about princes and witches and sorcerers. Children will recognize the underlying truths in the stories, but not because the truths are preached at them. These are not sermons. They are tales to be enjoyed for the enchantment they can give to young minds.

Perhaps I should have started this introduction not with "Tell me a story," but "Read me a story," since these stories will be read to many children. As a mother myself, I know that one of the greatest delights of parenthood comes at the time, usually at bedtime—before that third glass of water—when a parent reads and a child listens to a much-loved story. There is a closeness then between grown-up and child which seems to happen at no other time. I hope there will be many grown-ups and many children who will gain that lovely communion from this book.

MARTHA FOLEY

Table of Contents

Peter Ox

The old adage that "people believe what they want to believe" has never been more humorously demonstrated than in this old Danish folk tale. The author is unknown.

nce there lived in the region of Denmark known as Jutland a good-natured farmer and his pleasant wife, and you could have gone from east to west or from north to south without finding kinder, more honest folk. Never did they have a bad word to say about anyone or anything, and life was good on their large and prosperous farm. One day the farmer bought a fine calf, and he called it Peter, his favorite name.

Peter was a pretty calf, and seemed unusually bright. "He understands everything I say," the farmer proudly told his wife. "And Peter is also very friendly and polite."

The couple had no children, and they soon became as fond of Peter as if he had been their son. Indeed, one morning the farmer said to his wife: "I think that if we sent Peter to the town clerk, our calf could even be taught to speak. And if our Peter does learn to talk and write and read, he could eventually become our heir and would manage our farm."

"A fine idea," his wife replied. "The clerk is such a clever person that he might really succeed in teaching our Peter to speak."

That very afternoon the farmer went to the clerk and revealed his plans. Now this clerk was a sly and cunning man, and he did not—as you might expect—laugh at the farmer, or make fun of him. Instead he listened attentively, and nodded his head in agreement with all the farmer said. Then, looking around to make sure that no one was listening, he whispered: "It is quite possible that this can be done. But we must keep it our secret. No one must ever know that I am teaching a calf to speak—especially not the mayor, since it is forbidden to try to teach animals to talk."

When the farmer vowed that no one would hear a word of their plan, the clerk went on to say that he needed several pieces of gold. "First," he explained, "I must purchase five special and expensive schoolbooks for our pupil."

"Perfectly all right," said the farmer. "If you will teach Peter to speak, I don't care how much I need to pay for his education."

They then arranged for the farmer to bring the calf to the clerk at night, so that nobody would see the animal enter his house.

After a week had passed, the farmer decided to visit Peter and see how his education was progressing. But the clerk wouldn't let the farmer near his calf, claiming that the poor animal would become homesick and would promptly forget everything he had already learned. "But," he assured the farmer, "Peter is learning even faster than could be expected."

Before the farmer left, the clerk asked for another piece of gold. "I must buy three new books for our scholar," he declared. "Gladly," replied the farmer, and when he left for home, his heart was filled with great hopes and expectations.

A week later the farmer again went to inquire about Peter's progress. "Our work is coming along as well as can be expected," he was told.

"Has my calf learned to say anything yet?"

"He certainly has," the clerk replied enthusiastically. "He keeps saying 'meh, meh'."

"Oh, the poor little animal must be ill," exclaimed the farmer, "and he must be asking for *mead*. All that talking must have made his throat sore—and honey will be good for him. I'll go out and buy some immediately."

Later that day the farmer returned with a full jug of mead, and gave it to the clerk; and still later that day, the clerk drank the delicious honey himself, and gave Peter milk instead—which was certainly better for the calf, in any event.

A few weeks passed without another visit from the farmer, who feared that it would cost him another gold piece were he to show up. He didn't mind paying for Peter's education, but he didn't want to become penniless doing it, either.

The clerk in the meantime had been feeding the calf the very best grains. Naturally enough, he had never bought even one book, knowing full well that an animal cannot be taught to speak, read or write. When the calf was nice and fat, the clerk slaughtered it, salted it, and put it away. Then he dressed in his formal robes and went to visit the farmer and his wife. "Good day," said this deceitful man. "Weren't you delighted by the way Peter spoke when he came home?"

"Good grief," cried the farmer excitedly, "Peter isn't here! Isn't he with you? He hasn't run away, has he?"

"I certainly trust that he hasn't done that," replied the sly clerk, speaking in shocked tones. "Not after all the effort, trouble and even money I've invested in him. No, I don't think Peter would do such a thing, particularly now, when I've actually taught him to talk. No," he repeated, shaking his head, "Peter wouldn't be as bad as that, or as inconsiderate."

"Well then, what happened?" asked the farmer nervously.

"This morning Peter told me that he longed to visit his parents. I thought this was a splendid idea, but since I wasn't sure that he'd be able to find his way home, I got dressed and intended to accompany him. When we reached the gate of my house, I realized that I'd forgotten my walking cane. I went back to get it, but when I returned Peter was no longer there. I assumed that he had gone ahead, but since he isn't here, I haven't the slightest idea where he might be."

Imagine how distressed the farmer and his wife were to hear this! Now, after their fondest hopes and dreams had apparently come

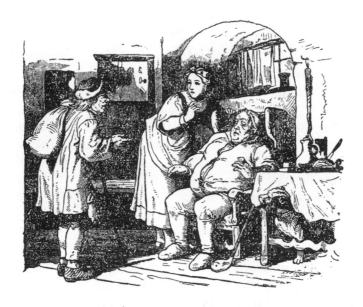

true—after they had invested so much money—Peter had run away. And worst of all, they were back where they had started: *they still had no heir*.

The clerk pretended that his sorrow was as deep as theirs. His moans were as loud as their moans; his sighs and sobs just as melancholy. "Perhaps," he sniffed, "Peter has only lost his way. Don't give up hope," he sighed. "We'll ask the pastor to mention Peter at church next Sunday. Maybe one of the parishioners will have seen our stray calf wandering about the countryside."

Then the cunning old rascal returned home and enjoyed a dinner of roast veal.

Not long after, the clerk heard that a merchant by the name

4

of Peter Ox had arrived in town. He was off at once to see the farmer and his wife. "It seems to me," he said, "that this person is perhaps none other than your own lost Peter calf."

"Of course," cried the farmer happily. "Who else could it possibly be?"

And his wife, who was equally delighted, immediately added: "Husband, you must visit him this very afternoon. Make sure that this Peter Ox is our Peter. And take a lot of money with you, husband, for if he is really our Peter and he has become a merchant, there's no doubt that he will need some capital."

The farmer quickly filled a purse with silver and gold, and journeyed to the city. When, panting and puffing, he reached the place where the new merchant lived, he smiled triumphantly.

I recognize him, the farmer said to himself. *I certainly recognize him! He has the same broad forehead that Peter had, the same thick throat and strong neck, and the same red hair!* But to the farmer's puzzlement, Peter now looked like a real man.

Then he said aloud to the merchant, "Oh, Peter, you gave us such heartaches when you ran away. We were so worried about you."

The merchant listened in complete astonishment. He had never, of course, seen the farmer before. Certain that he was confronted by a lunatic, he decided to avoid any discussion or argument.

"Now I really see how clever our town clerk is," the farmer continued. "He even taught you to *look* like a man, not just to talk and read and write. If I didn't know for sure that you are the calf we got from the red cow, I'd swear that you were like any other man. Are you ready to come home with me now, son?"

"No," said the merchant, searching for some way to end the incredible discussion. "I cannot do that, for I have some very important business appointments."

"Well, don't forget that the farm is waiting for you," replied the farmer. "As a matter of fact, as soon as you arrive, my wife and I will retire. But, of course, if you'd rather stay in business for a while, that's all right. Is there any way I can help you? Is there anything you need?"

"Well," said the mystified merchant, "in business one can always use more money."

"That's exactly what I thought. After all, Peter, when you started out just a few months ago, you had nothing at all. So I brought some money with me." And he emptied his purse on the table.

The clinking of the coins brought smiles of friendship and hospitality to the merchant's face. "Good farmer," he chortled, "I'll forget my business appointments. Stay on and have tea with me."

"I'll be glad to stay," the farmer replied. "But from now on you must call me father."

"But I have neither father nor mother."

"Oh, I know that," said the farmer. "Your father, the fine brown ox, was sold a few months ago, and your mother, the red cow, went with him. But my wife and I decided to adopt you as our child, so now you are our heir. Therefore you must call me father."

The merchant smiled benevolently. "All right, father. It will be a pleasure to call you by that name."

Eventually Peter Ox and the farmer went to share their joy with Peter's "mother." It was the happiest day of her life, said she, when she learned that Peter Ox was none other than their calf.

The couple then sold their farm, and moved to the city, where Peter Ox lived. And Peter, thinking of the large fortune that would someday be his, treated the old couple as tenderly as if they were his real parents.

And before long he genuinely learned to love them. Thus all three—and even the sly old clerk—lived happily to the end of their days. Happiness, like God's rain, may sometimes fall on good and bad alike.

The Pastor and the Sexton

A pastor not fit for his duties is taught a lesson in this popular Norwegian folk tale, dating from the 18th century, later retold by Asbjornsen and Moe.

There was once a pastor so impressed with himself—so "stuck up," everyone said—that whenever he walked down a road he bellowed, "Make way for the pastor, make way for the pastor!" And all the people and all the carts and all the carriages and wagons moved to one side so that the pastor might have the entire road to himself.

One day while walking on the main road the pastor noticed a particularly elegant carriage approaching. "Make way for the pastor," he shouted. "Make way for the pastor!" The pastor did not realize it, but he was now calling orders to the royal coach of the king!

The king was distressed and displeased to see so vain a person in a position of such importance. He ordered his carriage halted at once. And when the pastor saw the king's angry expression, he bowed his head in shame and fear.

"Pastor," the king said, "come to my castle tomorrow. Unless you can answer the three questions I will ask you, you shall be removed from your post."

The pastor was now frightened and upset, for he knew only how to bluster and shout. Giving reasonable answers to questions was a different matter altogether. He was determined to find a way out of his predicament, though, and he thought hard about this for three hours. At last he had an idea.

"I will go to the sexton," he decided. "He has a reputation for being both thoughtful and reasonable. Perhaps he will go to the palace in my place."

The two men discussed the matter, and finally the sexton agreed to the pastor's proposal.

Early the next morning, the sexton—dressed in the pastor's robes—went to the castle.

"Let us begin immediately," the king said. "Tell me, pastor, how far is it from East to West?"

"It is one day's journey, your majesty," the sexton replied.

"Why is that, pastor?"

"Because, your majesty, the sun rises in the East and sets in the West, and it makes the trip in but one day."

"That is good," the king said. "You have answered the first question correctly. Now tell me how much I am worth, just as I stand here before you?"

"That I can also answer readily," the sexton replied. "Christ was valued at thirty pieces of silver, and no matter how much I might like to, I could not possibly put your value at more than twenty-nine pieces of silver."

"That is true," the king said. "Now, pastor, since you are so very clever, can you tell me what I am thinking of at this moment?"

"Your majesty," the sexton smiled, "you think that a pastor is standing before you. But you are wrong, for I am really only his sexton."

"In that case," said the wise king, "go back to your church at once. You shall be the pastor from now on, and the arrogant pastor will be your sexton."

Lars, My Servant

*This classic 17th century fairy tale from Sweden,
telling the story of a man who wanted too much,
is a great favorite throughout Europe. The author
is unknown.*

There once was a duke who did not enjoy living in a palace. Nor did he like the idea of ruling his dukedom. Therefore he did neither. Instead he roamed the world, and wherever he went he was always welcomed, since this young duke was also very rich and generous. He loaned or spent or gave his money freely, never even bothering to keep count of his wealth. Then one day to his great surprise he realized that he had spent his entire fortune. He didn't have even a penny left in his purse. But what surprised him even more was that all those people he had so royally entertained in the past now ignored him. And when he tried to collect money from those to whom he'd loaned it, they just laughed at him.

So there he was, all alone in a foreign land, and deserted by his former friends. He gave his situation careful thought and then decided that he would make his way home on foot, begging for a coin or a piece of bread wherever he could.

Late one night he came to an immense forest. He gathered fern, moss and pine needles to make the ground as comfortable as possible. Then just before he fell asleep he noticed an old hut behind some shrubbery. Thinking that even an old and drafty shack would be more comfortable and would afford more protection from the cold wind than did his outdoor bed under the trees, he arose and entered.

The shack was completely empty except for an enormous box that stood against the wall. Curious to find out if anything of value was in it, the duke opened the box. But all he found inside was another box. And inside that one, yet another. And so on, each box being smaller than the previous one. Finally he came to the very last. It was only half an inch long, half an inch wide, and half an inch deep. Hoping that inside that box there might at least be a gold coin, he was very discouraged when all he found was an old, crumpled piece of paper.

He was about to throw the wad of paper away when he noticed that something was written on it. Slowly he spelled out the words and read, "Lars, my servant!"

No sooner had he muttered these words than he heard a voice close to his ears, "What does the master command?"

The duke looked around but could see no one. "That's odd," he thought, and he read the words once again. "Lars, my servant!"

And exactly as before there came the reply, "What does the master command?"

"If there is someone here who hears my voice, he might have the kindness to get me something to eat," the duke said. Instantly, a table piled high with the finest of foods appeared in the hut.

He sat down and ate and drank to his heart's content. When he had consumed all he could he again reached for the paper.

"Lars, my servant."

"What does the master command?" came the by-now-familiar reply.

"Since you have given me food and drink you should also get me a comfortable bed in which to sleep. And be sure that it is a very good bed, for I am accustomed to only the finest."

And so it happened. A moment later there stood in the hut

a bed so elegant and beautiful and covered with the finest eider downs that it was indeed fit for a king. For the moment the duke was satisfied. But as he lay down he thought that the hut was really too shabby for such a beautiful bed.

"Lars, my servant," he called out.

"What does the master command?"

"You have provided me with an excellent meal and a fine bed. Now I think I should have a better home. I am a duke, you see, and am used to living in a castle decorated with brilliant tapestries and golden mirrors." The moment he finished speaking there rose about him the most marvelous room he had ever seen. And since he was now both comfortable and satisfied, he at last turned over on his side and fell asleep.

When the duke awakened the next morning, he arose and looked about him. To his astonishment, the mysterious Lars had not only furnished one room, but had created a sixty-five-room castle. Ornate furniture was neatly arranged in every room. Oriental rugs covered the floors. Frescoes and oil paintings decorated the walls. Looking out one of the sparkling windows, the duke saw beautiful gardens, carefully trimmed trees and exotic flowers in bloom. Whereupon he again took his precious paper. "Lars, my servant," he said.

"What does the master command?"

"You have given me a magnificent castle and I will stay here, for it suits me well. However, I must also have men and maids to serve me."

And so it happened. Instantly there arrived a group of servants and maids of all sorts—gardeners, cooks, scullery girls, butlers and even stableboys. The duke contentedly settled down to a comfortable and easy life.

But he didn't know that on the other side of the forest there was another castle in which lived the king who owned the forest, the fields and even the grounds on which the duke had erected his castle. When the king arose that morning and looked out his window, he saw a sight he couldn't believe. For there before him was a castle with a glistening golden roof—*where nothing had been the day before!* He thought that he was still asleep and dreaming, and returned to his bed. When he arose again a few minutes later he threw cold water on his face, to make sure that he was fully awake, and then he walked to the window again. The castle was, of course, still there.

"Unbelievable," the king muttered to himself. And then he

called for his courtiers, who came running at his command.

"Do *you* see a castle over there?" the king asked in unbelieving tones, pointing a finger in the direction of the castle.

The courtiers' eyes grew as wide as saucers. Yes. They certainly saw it.

"Who has dared build such a castle on my grounds?" the king demanded of his lord chancellor.

The chancellor bowed low, remarking that the weather was indeed splendid. He knew nothing about the castle, and desperately wanted to change the conversation. But the king would not be distracted. He next called his generals, and said to them: "Send out all my foot soldiers and my cavalry and tear that castle down. And then bring me the man who built it."

To the sound of trumpets and the beat of drums, the soldiers marched off.

The duke heard the trumpets and the drums long before he saw the army approaching his castle. Recognizing the trumpet blares as a call to battle, he reached for the paper.

"Lars, my servant," he said calmly.

"What does the master command?"

"There are soldiers coming to attack me. You must get me twice as many soldiers as are crossing the forest. Also bring me weapons and whatever else is needed. But be quick about it."

And quick it was. When the duke looked out the window he saw that Lars had placed a huge army around his palace. When the king's men approached and saw the size of the duke's fighting force, they dared not advance.

The duke, who was a courageous soldier, then mounted a horse, and rode directly to the king's commander. "Why do you come toward us ready for battle?" he challenged.

The general told the duke his orders.

"This will never do," replied the duke. "You can see how many men I have. You will fight a hopeless battle. But if the king listens to me, we can become friends and I will help him against his enemies."

The general welcomed this proposal, and with his officers rode to the duke's castle. There they talked about all sorts of things, and in the course of the conversation the duke learned that the king had an extraordinarily wise, witty and beautiful daughter. However, confided the general, she did have one great fault: she was so extremely vain and proud that she had not as yet met a man she considered sufficiently good for her.

"Well, if it's nothing worse than that," the duke laughed, "I am not worried. This is something I know how to cure very easily."

Thus talking and laughing, the new friends passed many hours. But soon night came—time for the king's army to return. The general thanked the duke for his hospitality, and left with his staff. Behind them marched the king's soldiers, proud to have avoided bloodshed and to be bringing with them the duke's message of friendship and loyalty to the king.

Now that the duke was alone, he thought about the princess. If she was really as talented and lovely as the general said she was, he wanted to marry her. And as so many wonderful and unusual things had already happened to him that day, the duke felt that this wish might also come true.

"Lars, my servant," said he.

"What does the master command?"

"As soon as the king's daughter has fallen asleep, you must bring her here. But take care that she does not wake up. Do you understand?"

Less than an hour passed. Then suddenly the sleeping princess was magically transported to the duke's palace—still in the chair in which she had fallen asleep, still with a book open on her lap. She was even more beautiful than the general had said, and the duke promptly fell in love with her.

"Lars, my servant," he called.

"What does the master command?"

"Take the princess home again. Tomorrow I shall pay my respects to the king and ask him for his daughter's hand."

The next morning when the king arose he rushed to his window to see if his orders had been carried out and the castle destroyed. But to his great annoyance it still gleamed and glittered in the bright sun. At first the king was so flabbergasted that he didn't know what to say. Never before had one of his orders been disobeyed.

"This must be the work of the devil," he finally mumbled. His face reddened with anger and he shouted for his courtiers. They came running in great haste, bowing low before their sovereign.

"Do you still see a castle over there?" shouted the king. They craned their necks, opened their eyes as wide as saucers, and nodded.

"Didn't I order you to tear that castle down and bring me the villain who built it?" the king demanded.

Again they nodded their heads. But now the general stepped forward and told the king that the duke's army was at least twice as large as his army, and that a battle would have been hopeless. Then the general extended the duke's greetings and expression of friendship. When the king heard of the size of the duke's army he grew so dizzy that he had to take off his crown and put it on the table. Then he scratched his head. Even though he was a king and a very wise one, he could not understand the strange events of the last two days. How could anyone build a castle in a single night? How could so powerful an army be assembled so suddenly? And when he couldn't answer these questions, he decided that the duke was either the devil himself or a mighty sorcerer. While he sat on his throne trying to decide what to do, scratching his head in a most thoughtful manner, the princess entered.

"Good morning, dear father," she said. "Last night I had the strangest and most beautiful dream."

"What did you dream, dear girl?" the king asked.

"Oh, I dreamed that I was at the new castle, and that I found the duke to be more splendid and handsome than I ever imagined a man could be. And now, father, I want this duke as my husband."

"What?" shouted the king. "You who never even deigned to look at a man, you want as a husband a man you have never seen? This is most peculiar."

"That may be," said the princess, "but that's the way it is. I want a husband, and it is the duke I intend to marry."

At that moment the trumpets blared in the courtyard, announcing the arrival of the duke and a large entourage of men and women, all splendidly dressed in costumes of gold and silver.

The duke greeted the king most politely. The king replied in kind. And as they talked about affairs of state, they became great friends, and the king ordered that a banquet luncheon be celebrated in the duke's honor. At the table the duke was seated next to the princess. What they talked about nobody knows, but from the lady's radiant smile it was clear that she enjoyed every word the duke uttered. At the end of the banquet the duke asked the king for his daughter's hand in marriage. Although the king didn't want to say *no*—because he realized that it was to his advantage to have so powerful a man as the duke for a friend—he felt that he couldn't possibly say *yes,* until he had seen the duke's castle and had learned more about him.

It was decided, therefore, that the king and his daughter

would visit the duke that very afternoon. The duke hurried home and told Lars to prepare the palace for the royal visit. When the king and the princess arrived they were overwhelmed by the exquisite beauty of the castle and by the splendor of the surrounding grounds.

Then the king told the duke that he would be honored and delighted to have him as his son-in-law and future ruler of his kingdom.

The wedding was celebrated the next day, and the duke returned to his palace with his beautiful young wife. Everything he could possibly have wished for had come true, and he was very happy.

A few days later, in the middle of the night, the duke heard someone whispering to him.

"Is the master satisfied now?"

Though the duke could not see anyone, he knew that the speaker was Lars. As he sat up in his bed he again heard the same question: "Is the master satisfied now?"

"Quite satisfied, thank you," the duke replied. "You have given me everything I have ever wanted."

"But what have you given me in return?" asked Lars.

"Nothing," said the duke. "But what *can* I give you—you who are not flesh and blood—whom I cannot even see? If there is anything I can do for you, just tell me what it is and I will see that it is taken care of immediately."

"I would very much like to have the little piece of paper you have in the box," replied Lars.

"If that's all you want," said the duke, "you may have it. Certainly I don't need the paper any more, because by this time I know the words by heart."

Lars thanked the duke and instructed him to lay the paper on the chair next to his bed. He said that he would pick it up later that night.

The duke did exactly as he was asked to do and went back to sleep. Towards morning he woke up because he was so cold that his teeth were chattering. And to his horror he realized that he was again in rags, and that instead of lying in his comfortable bed in the beautiful

15

bedroom, he was lying on the big box in the old hut.

At once he cried, "Lars, my servant!" But there was no reply. He called a second time, "Lars, my servant!" But again there was no answer. He shouted for Lars as loudly as he could. But it was all in vain. Lars did not appear.

Slowly he realized what had happened. When Lars had taken the crumpled piece of paper, he had also freed himself of the magic spell that required him to do the bidding of anyone who held the paper in his hand. And he, the duke, had been foolish enough to help him do it.

Well, the duke wondered, what now? He was back in the old hut. His wife was still beside him, and still asleep, but he could see her shiver and tremble from the cold. He awakened her. And he explained everything to her. He told her that she was free to leave him. She reminded him of the vows they had taken together at the wedding, and said that she would not desert him in his time of trouble and need.

The next morning the king awoke in good spirits and walked to the window to gaze again at the wondrous castle of his son-in-law. But now he couldn't spy a trace of it! He frantically rang for his courtiers, who rushed to his room, bowing deeply.

"Do you see a castle over there beyond the forest?" the king asked.

Nobody saw a thing.

"Then what happened to it?" the king asked. But nobody had the faintest idea.

The king decided to investigate the mystery at once. And just as he had done a day earlier, he crossed through the forest. But when he reached the place where the castle and its great park should have been, he found nothing but pine and juniper trees. Then in the thick shrubs he noticed a broken-down little hut that he had never seen before.

The sight that greeted the king when he opened the door to that tiny hut startled him so that he couldn't move or speak. Standing before him was his son-in-law, dressed in rags; and seated on a box was his daughter, weeping.

"What is the matter? What has happened?" the king shouted. But he received no reply, for the duke had sworn to himself that he would rather die than tell the king his strange and unbelievable story.

The king questioned him at length. First in a friendly manner,

16

it must be said; then, when he received no answer to any of his questions, angrily. But the duke was stubborn and refused to talk.

The king then became furious, and ordered that the duke be hanged immediately. And no matter how plaintively his daughter begged him to show mercy and save her husband's life, the king's mind was made up.

So the soldiers set up the gallows and put a rope around the duke's neck. But while they were erecting the gallows the princess whispered to the hangman, offering him a purse of gold if he would help her save the duke. The hangman had a fondness for shiny gold pieces, and promptly agreed to cut the rope as soon as the king left the scene. In that way, the hangman assured the princess, the duke would not die, but would only suffer some discomfort.

The duke, however, felt certain that his end had come. He reflected on his past foolishness—first, for having wanted too much; and second, for having given Lars the precious little piece of paper. *If I could only hold that little paper now*, he thought, *I would show everybody that I have learned my lesson!*

And as he dangled there on the gallows, expecting each breath to be his last, he heard a terrifying laugh. When he looked down he saw an ox pulling seven carts, each piled high with worn-out shoes. In the driver's seat atop the first cart sat a tiny man dressed in grey. On his head he wore a peaked hat. His face was wrinkled and aged and the color of his flesh was transparent and ghostlike. He drove straight up to the gallows, and when he was directly before it, he stopped his carts. Then he looked up at the duke and laughed.

"Well, my dead friend," he cackled, "so that's where your story ends—at the gallows." And he laughed again. "Yes, my good duke," he continued, "there you hang, and here I drive off with seven carts of old shoes that I wore out running your errands for you. Now Lars is ready to give you your paper again—now that you can't even see it!" And the old man laughed again, and waved the paper under the duke's nose.

But not all are dead who hang from the gallows, and this was the mistake that old Lars made. For the duke reached out suddenly, and grabbed the paper from the little man's hand.

"Lars, my servant!" he shouted.

"What does the master command?" came the reply.

"Cut me down from the gallows and restore the castle exactly as it was. And when it grows dark, bring back the princess."

It happened. Within an hour all was as before.

When the king awakened the next morning he peered out of the window as usual. There stood the castle again, its golden roof glittering beautifully in the sunlight. "Impossible!" he said aloud, and held his head between his hands. Then he called for the courtiers.

"Do you see a castle there?" asked the king.

They craned their necks and stared. "Yes, yes," they all said. "Yes, we see the castle."

The king then sent for the princess, but she was not in the castle. Next the king rushed over to the gallows to make sure that his son-in-law was dead, but he could find neither gallows nor son-in-law. Again the king was so puzzled that he took off his crown and scratched his head. But that did not change anything. Nor could he understand these strange events.

At last he set out with his entire court toward the castle of the duke. And when he reached the great hall of the palace, the duke and his wife came down the stairs, dressed in their finest clothes. They calmly greeted the king.

This can only be the work of the devil! thought the king.

"Good day and welcome, father," said the duke.

"Are you really my son-in-law?" the king demanded.

"Yes, of course," replied the duke, "who else should I be?"

"Didn't I have you put away yesterday, like a common thief?" asked the king.

"Tut, tut," said the duke. "I rather believe that father has lost his wits. Does he really believe that I would let myself be hung like that? Is there anyone here who believes that?" And the duke stared icily at his people.

They bowed low and shook their heads.

"Or is there anyone in this great hall," the duke continued, "who dares to say that the king is my enemy?" And again the duke glared at the people, this time even more sternly than before.

Again they bowed and murmured, "No, sire, no!"

"I didn't think that anybody would be that foolish," said the duke.

Now the poor king was totally confused. He no longer knew what to think or whom to believe. When he looked at the duke's demeanor and noble bearing he felt that he could never have done anything unpleasant to him. Yet yesterday's image was so real: the shack,

18

the duke in rags, his daughter crying. Perhaps it was all a nightmare! He was determined to get to the bottom of it.

"Tell me, son-in-law," he said, "when I came here yesterday, didn't I find you standing in rags in a shack?"

The duke laughed. "What our father won't say today!" he finally commented, turning to his wife. "I do believe the trolls must have led him astray in the forest and confused his mind. What do you think?" he asked, turning to the court.

Everybody nodded his head to show agreement with the duke.

The king rubbed his eyes. "Well, then, it must be as you say —I believe I have come to my senses now. For it would really have been too stupid of me to have had you hung."

And with that everybody became happy once more and not another word was said about the affair.

Now the duke had learned his lesson. He remembered the seven carts of shoes old Lars had worn out in his service, and he rarely called on him any more.

Then one day Lars came to the duke.

"Do you need my help any longer?" he asked. "You haven't called on me for months and I haven't needed a new pair of shoes in months. In fact, I almost feel as if moss were growing on my legs. Couldn't you let me go?" he begged.

The duke agreed. "I have taken great care to save your feet, and I am sure that I can do without you. But the castle and all the other things I cannot do without, and I shall never find another builder like you. You must certainly understand that I have no desire or intention ever to decorate the gallows again. Therefore, I will never give you back your little sheet of paper."

"As long as you have it, I am not worried," replied Lars. "But if the paper should fall into somebody else's hand, I would have to start running about again, and I really don't want to do that. You know, when one has done this work for more than a thousand years, one becomes very tired."

Lars and the duke discussed the matter in great detail. Finally they agreed that the duke should put the paper in a tiny box and bury it seven yards deep in a place that Lars could never reach. Furthermore, the duke promised Lars that he would never divulge the spot to anyone.

Then they thanked each other for their good company and parted.

The duke followed his agreement with Lars; he buried the paper and kept the place a secret. And he lived happily with his princess in his luxurious castle, and they had many children. When the old king died many years later the duke inherited the kingdom and became famous for his long and wise rule.

But it is said that many people still go into the forests near Stockholm looking for the place where the duke buried the slip of paper.

For you know, of course, that if you should ever find it, old Lars would be ready to bring you anything your heart desires. But please also remember not to make old Lars work too hard, because if you take advantage of him, things *could* go wrong—as they almost did for the duke.

More South than South, More North than North

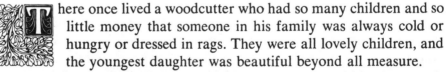

From the collection of the great Norwegian story-teller, P. C. Asbjornsen, a magical tale in the classic tradition of Scandinavian folklore.

There once lived a woodcutter who had so many children and so little money that someone in his family was always cold or hungry or dressed in rags. They were all lovely children, and the youngest daughter was beautiful beyond all measure.

One wintry day a fearful storm raged outside the wood-cutter's hut. It was dark and it was snowing, and the wind howled so fiercely that the house creaked in all its joints. The entire family clustered about the hearth trying to keep warm.

Suddenly they were startled by three loud raps on the door. Who could it be, so late at night and in such frightful weather? The woodcutter stepped outside. And there before him was a great white bear.

"Good evening," said the bear politely, speaking just as well as you or I.

"Good evening," the surprised woodcutter replied.

"I am here to make a bargain with you," continued the bear in courteous tones. "If you will give me your youngest daughter as my wife, I will make you as rich as you now are poor."

The father was pleased with this unusual proposal, but he wanted to discuss it with his daughter. He returned to the fireplace and told his daughter that a handsome, well-spoken white bear waited outside, ready to make them as rich as they now were poor. All she need do was consent to marry him.

"No, I can't do that," the frightened girl replied.

The father then went back to the waiting bear and told him to return in three days, at which time he would receive an answer.

For the next three days the girl's parents pleaded with her. They assured her that she had nothing to fear from this remarkable animal, who was kind and generous and would help them all in their need. And when the girl realized that her entire family seemed to want her to go off with the bear, she finally consented.

She washed and mended and pressed her clothes, packed them into neat little bundles, and prepared herself for the trip ahead. And when the bear arrived to fetch his bride, she seated herself, with all her belongings, on his back. They traveled in silence until the wood-cutter's hut was out of sight; and then the bear stopped and asked his new wife if she was afraid of him.

"No, not at all," she replied.

"That's good," replied the bear. "In that case just hold tightly to my fur, and I will run much faster."

This the girl did, and the bear ran so swiftly through forests, over mountains and rocky cliffs that they almost seemed to fly.

At last they came to a mountainside so steep, so vast, and so bare that further progress seemed impossible. The bear did halt; but then he touched the rock with his heavy paws—and a door opened—and in they went.

How astonished the girl was when she found herself entering not a dark and gloomy cave, but a magnificent, brilliantly illuminated castle. Crystal chandeliers with hundreds of twinkling candles hung in every room. And as the bear led his bride through the palace it seemed to her that each new room was more majestic than the one before it.

At last they came to a great hall that was completely empty except for one long, narrow, silver table. On it were piled hundreds of rubies, emeralds, diamonds and other precious stones, along with dazzling rings and diadems, golden crowns, scepters and other treasures.

The bear walked to the table and from it took a silver bell, which he gently held in his shaggy paw.

"Whenever you want anything," he said, "simply ring this bell, and you will instantly be given whatever you desire. But there is one request I must make of you."

"And what is that?"

"You must promise that you will never look at me while I sleep. Nor may you ever ask any questions about me."

And this she promised.

When night came and the girl lay down to sleep in her golden bed in a golden room, the bear came to bid her good night. To her astonishment she realized that he had changed into a man. But the next morning, alas, her husband was again a bear. Yet the promise she had made never to ask anything or anyone about him, or about the strange events of the past few days, prevented her questioning him about his sudden transformations.

Many months so passed. The girl and the bear lived happily in the castle. And as he had said, her slightest wish was fulfilled merely by ringing the magic silver bell.

Early each morning the bear left their castle, reappearing in the evening only after the sun had gone down. At home he was gentle and kind and loving; indeed, she was so completely devoted to him that she almost forgot that he was a bear.

But because she was alone all day, her thoughts turned always to her brothers and sisters, her mother and father, and to the forest in which they had lived. She wondered if she would ever see them

again. And when her husband understood how much she yearned for her parents, he told her that he would take her home for a brief visit.

"But there is one condition," said the bear. "You must promise me that you will not talk with your mother alone. Speak with her only when others are in the same room.

"She will probably take you by the hand," he predicted, "and she will insist that you sit privately with her. It will be then that the greatest danger exists. For if you yield to her entreaties and go with her to the private room, you will bring unhappiness on us both."

The next day, so early that the dark colors of the night still lingered in the sky, the girl and the bear began their journey. He ran so fleetly that they reached her parents' home in a twinkling. It had changed so much, however, that the girl didn't recognize it. Instead of a house with a rotting patched roof, peeling sides and broken windows, there stood a splendid mansion surrounded by rose gardens and a fish pond. Only when she saw her sisters walking in the garden did she know that this was really her parents' home.

"Here we are," said the bear. "But don't forget what I told you, for if you do you will surely bring unhappiness on yourself and on me."

"I won't," promised the girl, and joyfully she ran through the gate, across fine lawns decorated with fountains and statues, and down a marble path into her parents' home.

How delighted they were to see her again! How grateful for what she had done for them! And how pleased when she assured them that the giant white bear had made her very happy, and that she had everything a young wife could possibly want.

But after lunch, things began to happen just as the bear had predicted. Her mother wanted to speak to her alone, and tried to lead her into another room. Remembering her husband's strange words of warning, the girl refused: "Whatever we have to discuss with each other we say right here," she said. But her mother was so persistent, so insistent that eventually the girl yielded. And when they were all alone, she then could not resist further temptation, and she revealed all she knew about the bear—the mysterious castle concealed in a bleak mountain cliff, the lavish treasures of his home, the wondrous silver bell—and even the fact that he changed into a man night after night. When her astonished mother asked what he looked like—whether he was old or young, fat or thin, tall or short, handsome or ugly—she confessed that she had never seen him.

"Then take this candle," urged the mother, "and hide it under your bodice. And at night, when he is sound asleep, light the candle, and you will be able to see your husband's face. But be careful that no drops of wax fall and awaken him, for this might make him angry."

The daughter took the candle and concealed it. That evening, when the bear came to take her back to the palace, he peered questioningly, silently, deeply into his wife's eyes: when she turned away in embarrassment, tears showed in his huge, gentle, brown eyes. Sorrowfully he asked if things had gone as he had predicted. But the girl was too ashamed to admit that she had broken her promise, and she did not reply.

Then the bear said, "If you follow your mother's advice, and do what she suggested, all will be over, and we will both be most unhappy."

"I shall certainly not follow my mother's advice," she answered, and she meant every word of her promise. But that same night, once she knew that her husband was asleep, she couldn't resist temptation. With trembling fingers, she lit the candle; and there in the flickering golden light was the most handsome man she had ever seen. His face was so kind, so gentle that she could not resist the wish to kiss him once. But as she leaned over, three drops of hot wax fell on his shirt, and he awakened with a start.

"What have you done?" he cried. "Oh, now you have brought misery on us both. Had you been patient for but a year I would have been freed from this horrible curse forever. But now all is over. I must go back to the evil troll who enchanted me. She lives in a castle more north than north and more south than south. And there I must marry her daughter, the giantess with a nose four yards long."

The girl wept, of course, and lamented, but this did not help. He could do nothing but leave her. She asked if she might not accompany him, for she loved him so dearly that she wanted to be with him even in his misery.

"No," he replied, "that you are not allowed to do."

"But then at least tell me the way to the castle, so that I can search for you."

"I can tell you the way," he replied, "but you will never find me, for the castle lies more north than north and more south than south. No, not in a lifetime can you get there, for if only once you rest or even bend your legs to sit, in that same moment you will be as far behind as you came forward in one day. And the castle is so far away that you cannot get there without resting."

No sooner had he said these words than before her eyes he turned into a bear again, and ran from the room.

"It will do no good to cry," thought the unhappy girl. "It will do no good to stay here. It will do no good to return to the home of my parents. And so I will search for my husband, come what may."

All she took with her for her journey was a ball of wool, a length of cotton and a length of linen cloth, thinking that these materials would prove useful when she wore out her clothes.

She walked the entire day, until her feet ached and her spirits were low. But she could not stretch out to sleep, nor even sit to rest. Instead, when the sun set, she climbed onto a high tree and wedged herself between two branches in such a way that she could neither sit nor bend her legs. When the moon rose a pack of wolves appeared and surrounded her tree, howling so ferociously and baring their fangs so fiercely that the poor girl was cold with fear and terror. But with the very first ray of the sun, the wolves dispersed.

The next day she wandered farther and deeper into the forest, over thorns and splintery rocks, until she pained so that she could scarcely take one more step. Nevertheless she dragged herself forward until sundown, and then climbed another tall tree. Throughout the long night she clung to its branches with both arms so that she would neither be able to sit nor bend her knees. When the moon rose a band of bears gathered around the tree trunk, growling and menacing her, and before long they even tried to climb up to her, forcing her to climb to the highest part of the tree. Yet again, as soon as day broke, the beasts dispersed.

Then she descended and continued her search, covering an even greater distance than on the previous day. At night, she once more climbed a tree, and scarcely had she reached the lowest branch when ten snarling, snapping lions appeared. All night their fearful roaring echoed from cliff and forest, and they leaped so hungrily that the earth shook. Failing in their attempt to climb the tree, the lions desperately clawed the ground, trying to unearth the tree's roots and thus make it fall. The poor girl clung to the highest branch in terror, but she did not sit or bend her knees, nor did she even dare think about sleep. At last day dawned and the lions vanished.

But now as she resumed her exhausting journey, the woodcutter's daughter wept as she walked. She did not know where she was, for although she had sought in north and south, in east and in west, she had not found the place more south than south and more north than north, nor had she seen even a trace of the bear who was her husband.

That night she came to a great cliff, much like the magical palace she had known, and thinking that perhaps someone lived here, she rapped on the rock until her knuckles were bruised. And then she heard a voice from within:

"Who is making all that fuss?"

It was a loud, rough voice, and it seemed to come from a crack in the cliff. It was followed by a nose almost one yard long. And at last came the head of a giantess. "Who are you?" she bellowed. "Why do you wake me?"

"I am a poor wanderer," the girl replied, "and I am seeking my husband. He is in a place more north than north and more south than south. Can you show me the way?"

"Fie," screamed the giantess. "That is far, far away. One can neither sail there nor row there. And no one has yet reached it on foot. You are wasting your time, and you might just as well go home now as later. For even if you do get there, you will be too late. Your husband must now marry the giantess with a nose four yards long."

But the girl would not turn back. "May I at least spend the night in your cave?" she begged.

"I can put you up, to be sure," the giantess replied, "but when my husband comes home and finds you he will bite off your head and eat you."

"I will take that chance, because I am too tired to walk any farther. And for your kindness, let me give you this." And the girl took from her bundle the ball of wool she had carried with her, and offered it to the giantess.

"How beautiful! How soft!" the giantess whispered. "I have been married for over a hundred years and have never possessed any wool."

She was so delighted that she comforted the girl and served her food. "Gobble it down quickly," she ordered. "My husband will soon be here. It is best if you hide in the storeroom. Perhaps he will not think to look there."

In the storeroom, behind great stacks of barrels and boxes, the giantess arranged a bed as soft as clouds. But as tired as she was, the girl dared not lie on it or even sit on it. In fact, she did not even close her eyes, since she had to take care not to bend her knees. Thus, she stood next to the tempting bed all night long, so miserable and weary that she could hardly bear it.

In the middle of the night she heard a frightful thundering and rattling. The troll had come home.

"Fee, fie, fo," he boomed. "I smell Norwegian blood." And he rushed about so wildly that sparks flew.

27

"Yes, yes," the giantess soothed him, "a bird flew past with the bone of a Norwegian and let it fall through the chimney. I threw it out as quickly as possible but some of the odor remains."

The troll was satisfied with her answer, and took his place at the table to eat his dinner. After he had consumed four roast bulls, drained six barrels of boiling tea, and eaten all the apples from all the trees in two orchards, he was in a pleasant mood. And so the giantess told her husband about the poor girl in the storeroom who had come through the forest in search of an enchanted bear in a place more north than north and more south than south.

"Oh fie, fie," the troll snorted. "That is so far away that one can neither sail there nor row there, and no one has yet gone there on foot. But where is the girl?" he demanded, and sniffed around everywhere.

"Can you do something for her?" the giantess asked. "She has given me a soft ball of wool. Will you lend her your seven league boots, so that she can quickly get to our nearest neighbor?" And because he was no longer hungry, and because the girl had given his wife a gift she loved, at last the troll agreed to help.

The next morning, after the girl had eaten breakfast and was ready to continue her trip, the troll directed her to slip on his seven league boots. "Now you have only to say *'Forward, over meadow and forest, over mountain and valley, to the nearest neighbor,'* and the boots will speed you there. And once you are there, just take the boots off and say: *'Where you were put on this morning, there you must rest tonight.'* And the boots will return to me instantly."

The girl followed the troll's instructions, journeying a mile with each step, high over mountains and across deep valleys, until, at sunset, she came to a vast grey cliff. There she took off the seven league boots and repeated the words the troll had recited: *'Where you were put on this morning, there you must rest tonight.'* And the boots flew away.

Then the girl rapped loudly on the cliff.

"Who is making all the commotion at my door?" came a screech from within. And through a crack in the cliff a giantess stuck out her nose, which was two yards long.

"I am a poor girl and I am looking for my husband. He is in a place more north than north and more south than south."

"Poor child," the giantess cried. "That is so far away that you can neither sail, nor row, nor walk there. Turn back now rather than later, for you are wasting your time."

But the girl refused to be discouraged. Instead she asked the giantess if she might stay in her cave for the night.

"You can stay, to be sure," the giantess replied, "but when my husband comes home tonight he will bite off your head and devour you."

Then the girl took the bolt of cotton she had carried with her, and gave it to the giantess. "How beautiful," cried the giantess. "I have now been married for over two hundred years, and have never before possessed cotton cloth." And she was so delighted that she invited the girl to dine with her. "But hurry," the giantess warned, "finish before my husband returns. I shall hide you in the storeroom, and let us hope that he does not find you, for he devours any Norwegian who passes here."

And again a bed was arranged for her, as soft as a puff of smoke, but the poor girl did not dare lie on it, nor even sit on it. No, she could not even close her eyes because then she might collapse on the bed or bend her knees. Thus she stood on her tired legs through the entire night, and was so miserable and weary that she could hardly bear it any longer.

After midnight she heard a terrible thundering and rattling. It was the troll. And scarcely had he stuck his head through the door than he bellowed, "Fee, fie, fo, I smell a Norwegian!" And he rushed about so furiously that sparks flew.

Then the giantess said that a bird had dropped a bone down the chimney, and that the scent still remained. This explanation satisfied the troll, who thereupon began his dinner of twenty-seven roast pigs, nine barrels of vinegar, and fish from five lakes. His appetite thus satisfied, he smiled happily. And so his wife dared tell him the truth.

"In fact," she concluded, "you should lend her your seven league boots so that she can reach our nearest neighbor by nightfall." This the troll agreed to do, and by evening the next day the girl had reached a dense forest where all the trees were coal black; just by occasionally brushing against their leaves she became as black and sooty as a chimney sweep.

In the middle of this strange forest she saw a clearing. And in the center of it stood a rotting, broken-down hut, held together by two shaky beams. In front of it was a heap of rubbish, a mountainous pile of torn old shoes, filthy rags and other ugly things. The woodcutter's daughter removed her borrowed boots and sent them back to their rightful owner, the troll.

Then standing before the door of the old hut—her clothes torn and her shoes worn to shreds, her face and arms and legs filthy from the walk through the black forest—standing there, looking poorer than the poorest beggar, she knocked on the door.

An ancient giantess with a nose four yards long stuck her head out of the window.

"If the woman at the door wants to come in, then she shall enter, but if she prefers to remain outdoors, then let her stay outdoors." Saying this the old giantess opened the door for an instant, and was about to slam it shut had the girl not cried out, "I want to come in."

Then the giantess offered her a drink of milk. "If the woman wants to drink, she may, but if she doesn't want to, she doesn't have to," she croaked. And the giantess would have taken the milk away, if the girl hadn't said, "Thank you, I would like to drink it."

Then the giantess gave her some moldy cheese and a crust of bread; the girl ate just enough to still her hunger, and then she thanked the giantess for her hospitality, and made ready to leave. But as she turned, she saw an old man lying on a bed of rags. His face was gloomy and lined with sorrow. Yet when she walked to him and reached for his hand, his face brightened.

"Listen to me," he whispered. "Now that you have come here, you should wash my shirt. The old giantess can never wash out the three spots of wax. Only a Norwegian can do that."

When the girl heard these words, she knew that the old man was indeed her husband. She rushed to the basin, where the giantess was scrubbing the shirt. "May I try?" the girl asked. The giantess did not reply; instead she scrubbed even more vigorously. But the longer she washed and scrubbed, the larger the spots became, and soon the shirt looked as ugly and black as if it had been used to clean a chimney.

"That's no good," said the man from his bed. "Let the beggar girl try to get it clean. Perhaps she knows more about washing than you do."

"All right, girl," said the giantess, "if you want to wash the shirt you may do so, but if you don't want to wash it, you don't have to."

"I want to wash the shirt," replied the girl immediately.

And the moment she dipped the shirt in the water it became as white as newly fallen snow.

When the giantess saw the clean shirt she became so angry and jealous that she burst in the middle and broke into two parts.

And as the old man got up from his bed of rags, he suddenly

changed back into the handsome young prince. In his hand he held the magic silver bell he had once given the girl in his castle.

He rang it and instantly he and the girl were back in their castle. But it was no longer located beneath a cliff; now it stood imposingly beneath a starry sky.

Then the prince told her that he would never become a bear again because the spell had forever been broken by her faith and courage. And so the two lived as prince and princess in good fortune and joy, until the end of their lives.

The King's Rabbits

"The boy who earns the right to marry a king's daughter" is a favorite fairy tale theme. This amusing Norwegian version, dating from the 17th century, is extremely popular throughout Europe.

 eter, Paul and Hans were the three idle sons of a wealthy merchant. Late each morning when they met at the breakfast table, Paul said:

"Nothing to do today but eat."

"And play," added Paul, the middle son.

"And then go back to sleep," concluded Hans, the youngest.

But one day Hans grew tired of this silly existence. "I want to find a job," he announced. "After all, most young men our ages work. Why shouldn't we?"

"What could we do?" asked Paul.

"The king needs a rabbit-keeper," replied Hans. "I plan to go to the king and ask for the post."

"You will not," snapped Peter. "I am the oldest. *I* will go to the king."

Without another word he dressed in his finest clothes and departed.

On his way to the palace, Peter passed an old woman whose nose was caught in a tree trunk. No matter how she pulled or tugged, she could not free herself. Peter had never concerned himself with other people's misfortunes, and he considered this sight most amusing. He stopped and stared and roared with laughter.

"Don't just stand there and laugh," cried the woman. "Come over and help me get loose. I am a weak old woman and I can't free myself. I came here one day to gather some firewood and instead I caught my nose in the tree. I have been here now for more than a hundred years, twisting and turning, but I'm still stuck. And I haven't eaten even a morsel of bread in all that time!"

Most people would help a poor woman who had suffered so. But not Peter. When he heard the story he laughed even louder. "If you've managed to stand there for a hundred years," he answered with a nasty chuckle, "you can certainly hold out for another hundred." Then he continued on his way.

When Peter arrived at the king's castle he was immediately hired as rabbit-keeper. "This is an unusual job," said the king. "The pay is high and the room in which you sleep is vast and beautiful. And if none of my rabbits escapes during the first three days, you can marry my lovely daughter. But if even one rabbit does run away or is stolen or sold, you will not only lose your job but be sent to sea for thirty years."

Early the first morning Peter led the king's rabbits to the pasture. There, to his great dismay, they instantly hopped off in all directions. No matter how he chased and clambered and called, they were far too quick to catch. Late that night when he returned to the palace without so much as one rabbit, the king was waiting. Peter was seized and sent to sea.

Paul heard of this, of course, and insisted that he be the next to try his luck. On his way to the palace he also came upon the old woman whose nose was stuck in a tree trunk. But Paul also just mocked her with nasty laughter, and refused to help in any way. Then, on the very first day he took the rabbits to the pasture, they scampered off to north, east, south and west—and when Paul returned empty-handed to the palace that evening, the king ordered him seized and sent to sea.

Now Hans decided to go to court and serve the king. Off he trudged toward the palace, and he too soon passed the unhappy old woman whose nose was caught in a tree trunk.

"Good day, mother," said Hans. "How did you manage to get yourself into such a fix?"

"No one has called me 'mother' for a hundred years," said the old woman. "You must be a kind lad. Well, then, please come over and help me get my nose out of this tree trunk. Perhaps you can also give me something to eat, for I haven't even munched a crumb of bread for a hundred years."

"Poor thing—if you haven't eaten in a hundred years, you must be painfully hungry," replied Hans.

Then off he rushed to borrow an axe; and when he returned, Hans split the trunk in half and freed the woman's nose. This accomplished, he opened his knapsack and shared his food with her.

When they had emptied the knapsack and licked their fingers, the grateful old woman reached deep in her pocket and pulled out a

whistle. "Here is a gift for you," said she. "Even though it looks quite common, it is by no means an ordinary whistle. If you blow on the small end, everybody and everything you want to see disappear will rush away from you. But if you blow on the large end, everybody and everything you want to return will speed right back."

"Indeed, this is a most extraordinary whistle," marveled

Hans. "Many thanks, good mother. I'm sure I'll find it useful."

Then the woman and Hans parted company, each taking a different road.

When Hans arrived at the castle and applied for the job, he was immediately hired.

The next morning the king took him to the yard where the rabbits lived in their golden hutches. When the doors were opened the rabbits dashed out and hopped toward the forest, disappearing into the woods even before Hans had passed through the courtyard gates.

The king smiled in sly triumph. "Another sailor for my ships," thought he. "Another sailor whom I need not pay."

But Hans was undisturbed. He chuckled at the agility of the rabbits, wished them a pleasant romp, and then happily wandered toward the forest. There he found a comfortable tree against which to rest, and soon fell sound asleep. When evening came and he awoke, not a single rabbit was in sight. Unperturbed, Hans took his whistle, placed it to his lips, and softly blew into it. Instantly and from all directions rabbits came hopping toward him. And when all had assembled around him, he led them to the castle, as easily as a shepherd brings home his flock of sheep.

"What's this?" cried the king when he peered out of his window and saw the boy returning with all the rabbits. "That new lad certainly knows a trick or two! But I'll fool him tomorrow, because I certainly don't want my daughter to marry anyone but a prince!"

The next day, when Hans was in the woods with the rabbits, the king sent the princess to visit him. To make sure that the lad would not recognize her, she disguised herself as a poor peasant girl. And in this costume she walked up to Hans and said, "Good shepherd, you have a great many rabbits. And since I need one badly, I would like to buy one from you."

But Hans wasn't fooled for a minute. He recognized the princess at once. "Alas," he replied, "the rabbits belong to the king. And if I lose even a small one, I will be sent to sea for thirty years. I know this all sounds very strange, but it's the law of the land, and there's nothing I can do about it."

"Oh, but I need a rabbit so very much," the princess begged. "If you don't give me one, I'll surely die. Certainly the king won't miss one little rabbit when he has so many."

"No, I cannot sell you one," Hans replied. "But if you want to earn one, that's a different story. All you have to do is kiss me."

34

Better to give him one kiss now, thought the king's daughter, *than to have a simple-minded boy instead of a prince as a husband for the rest of my life!* And so the princess went up to Hans and kissed him. In return Hans allowed her to choose a rabbit, and into her basket she placed it, thinking that Hans was now lost. He, however, climbed to the

top of a hill so that he could watch the princess walk toward the castle. When she had reached the edge of the forest, Hans blew his whistle. The rabbit leaped from the basket and came bounding back to him.

From the way the princess stamped her feet on the ground, Hans knew that she didn't at all like what had happened. Indeed, she returned to the palace in tears, and told her mother what had taken place.

"Don't worry, my dear," said the queen. "Tomorrow I myself will visit the boy, and you can rest assured that he won't trick me."

Bright and early the next morning the queen disguised herself as a peasant woman, even carrying a basket filled with eggs.

But when Hans saw her approach, he instantly recognized her.

"Good day, my son," she said. "I'm on my way to market to sell these eggs."

"Good day, mother," replied Hans, pretending that he didn't know who stood before him. "I hope you sell them for a fine, high price."

"My son," the queen continued, "I need a rabbit ever so badly. Would you be kind enough to sell me one?"

"I'm afraid I cannot," Hans replied. "It would be dishonest if I took money for something that doesn't belong to me. However, if you are willing to *earn* a rabbit rather than buy it, that might be all right."

"Splendid!" the queen replied with a smile. "We peasants try to save money whenever we can."

"Good," said Hans. "And I am sure that you won't find earning a rabbit difficult. All you need do is get down on your hands and knees and hop about like a rabbit."

"Why, that's outrageous," stammered the queen in horror.

"Not at all," replied Hans. "I think you'll find it fun."

This lad is a fool, thought the queen. *But since he doesn't know who I am, and since no one else is around, I might just as well go ahead and do as he asks.*

So down she went on all fours and hopped about like a rabbit.

"You have earned your rabbit," said Hans, wiping the tears of boisterous laughter from his eyes. "Go ahead and choose any rabbit you want."

The queen selected a small brown bunny, put it under her coat, and buttoned it tight. Then she turned without a word and started toward the city. Hans watched her carefully from his hill, and blew his whistle the moment she reached the edge of the forest. Instantly, the rabbit slipped from the queen's coat and raced back.

The king, in the meantime, anxiously awaited the arrival of the queen. "Well, did you succeed?" he asked her when she appeared. "No, no, no!" she sniffed. "I no sooner reached the edge of the forest than the rabbit jumped right out from under my coat and ran back."

"Hmmph!" snorted the king. "Neither you nor your daughter seems able to hold onto a rabbit. As usual, I have to do everything myself."

Early the next morning the king dressed in the leather breeches, high boots, shabby hat and long coat of a peasant. Then he mounted a donkey and rode off into the woods.

"Now I'll really have fun," said Hans to himself when he spied the rider and realized that he was none other than the king himself.

"My son," puffed the king when he reached Hans, "you must sell me a rabbit."

"And why is that?" asked Hans.

"Because you must," retorted the king, who was not at all used to having his commands questioned.

"I'm afraid I can't do that," replied Hans, "because the king will have me shipped to sea if I lose even a single rabbit. You may not know it, but that seems to be one of the ridiculous laws of this land."

"Ridiculous laws? In this land?" questioned the king, growing angry.

"Well, *I* think they're ridiculous. But there's no sense in discussing it. What's more, I'm sure you will agree that it wouldn't be honest for me to sell you something that belongs to the king."

"But I must have one," exclaimed the king. "And if you won't sell me a rabbit, I will certainly die. You don't want me to die, do you?"

"Indeed I don't," replied Hans. "Tell me, are you ready to work for a rabbit? That would be the one way I might let you have one."

"Certainly I'm ready to work for a rabbit," replied the king. "Just tell me what I must do."

"Oh, it's very simple. All you need do is kiss your donkey nine times on his nose."

It's worth it, thought the king, *to send this ninny off to sea! Suppose I had such a fool for a son-in-law! And since no one else but this worthless wretch will see me—and since he certainly does not recognize me—no harm will be done.*

"All right," said the king aloud. "I'll do it."

And nine times he kissed his donkey on the nose. In return, the laughing youth let him choose whichever rabbit he wanted. The king tied the animal to the inside of his coat. Then he buttoned the coat, buckled a belt around it, remounted his donkey and rode off without a word. Hans watched him and waited until the king reached the very steps of the castle. Then he placed the whistle to his lips and blew it as hard as he could. Instantly the rabbit wrenched itself free, burst the buttons of the king's coat, and leaped, hopped and bounded back to Hans.

"You see, it isn't so easy," cried the queen and the princess from their windows, secretly delighted at the king's misfortune.

That evening when Hans returned to the castle with all the rabbits, he went directly to the king.

"Your Majesty, I have done as you commanded," he said. "Now I ask you for your daughter's hand in marriage."

"Soon, my son, soon," the king replied. "Before you marry my daughter only one small task remains to be done. You must tell me enough stories to fill up a sack. In three days we will meet in the public square. And by that time you must be prepared to tell your stories. If you can't fill the sack, there'll be no wedding."

The king then ordered the royal tailor to sew a large woolen sack. Next, he commanded the court cabinet-maker to erect a frame in the marketplace from which the sack would be hung. And finally he commissioned the royal contractor to build a podium from which Hans would tell stories.

When the day came for Hans to begin his recitation, he climbed onto the podium. The king, queen and princess were seated on a first-row bench just below him. Behind them sat the ministers of state and other functionaries. And behind *them* stood hundreds of towns-people who had crowded into the square. Of all the people attending, none had dared ask how a sack could be filled with stories spoken into the air. None had been brave enough to point out that the king had given Hans an impossible task.

But Hans did not seem in the least dismayed. He greeted his audience with a smile, cleared his throat, and spoke: "Now I must begin to tell you enough stories to fill the sack. So listen very carefully. I will describe what happened while I was guarding the king's rabbits.

"The first day was a pleasant, easy one. I led the rabbits to the field, guarded them carefully, and returned at night with each and every one. The second day a pretty peasant girl came up to me. But, ladies and gentlemen, she wasn't actually a peasant girl at all. She was really the modest princess who is sitting right down there." And to the amusement of the crowd he pointed to her. Then he continued, "She begged me to sell her a rabbit. When I told her that I couldn't sell her something that didn't belong to me, she grew so sad and desperate that I suggested she could earn one just by giving me a kiss. And what do you think our princess did? Well, she pursed her little red lips and gave me a kiss. I then gave her a rabbit and she left with a smile on her lovely face. But apparently the rabbit didn't want to stay with her, because it soon hopped out of her basket and came back to me."

The crowd laughed; the princess blushed and hid her face in her hands. But the queen whispered in her ear, "Serves you right! That's what happens when you don't plan things properly. Your disguise was obviously no good."

Then Hans continued. "I can see that the sack isn't full yet, and so I shall continue with my stories. On the second day I had another visitor. An old peasant woman, on her way to market, spoke to me. But actually she wasn't a peasant woman at all. She was none other than our queen!"

"The rascal recognized me!" sputtered the queen in horror.

"Well," Hans continued, "she let me know soon enough that she also wanted a rabbit."

The queen turned beet-red with embarrassment, and implored the king to call an end to Hans' storytelling.

"Oh no," replied the king jovially. "The sack isn't full yet."

"I told Her Majesty," continued Hans, "that I couldn't possibly sell her a rabbit. But I added that if she wanted one badly enough, she could earn it by getting down on her hands and knees and hopping about like a bunny."

Loud laughter echoed through the square.

"And that," Hans said, "is exactly what our queen did. She puffed and panted, but I must admit that she did get down on all fours and start hopping around."

Now uncontrollable laughter swept the square. Tears even streamed down the king's cheeks.

"I then gave her majesty a rabbit, but apparently the bunny preferred me, because it soon jumped out from under her coat and returned."

Once again a wave of laughter resounded in the square.

"The fourth day," Hans continued, "was the best of all. For on that day our most gracious king visited me. He arrived riding on a donkey. He wore leather breeches, high boots, a long coat and a peasant's hat. He also wanted to earn a rabbit. I said to him, 'Kiss . . .'"

But Hans got no further.

"STO-O-OP!!!" shouted the king at the top of his voice. "The sack is full. In fact, it is overflowing. Come down, my son, you have earned the right to marry my daughter."

So Hans descended from the podium and walked to the princess. He apologized to her and together they returned to the castle. There he changed into princely garments, and when the princess saw that he was as handsome as he was clever, she fell in love with him.

They were married soon thereafter and lived happily and helpfully. And it is said that when Hans became king, he mounted the podium in the town's square once a year, and told stories to his subjects.

The Magic Storm

A young lad who saves a group of grown-ups from certain disaster is the classical theme of this story from Norway. The author is unknown.

 nce there was a cabin boy who sailed the Northern seas for three long years. When his ship finally returned to Oslo, his home, the boy told the captain that he had seen quite enough of the world, and had no intention of making another voyage.

The captain liked the cheerful and friendly lad, and was dismayed to hear that his cabin boy wanted no more of the seaman's life. But no matter how he tried to persuade the boy to change his mind, the captain did not succeed. The lad agreed only to stay aboard until new supplies and cargo were loaded into the holds.

On Sunday morning, the day before the scheduled departure of the vessel, the captain and his crew went ashore to spend the day with their families. The boy stayed on, as arranged, to serve as watchman.

As he paced the captain's bridge, he suddenly heard voices. This perplexed the lad, since he was supposed to be the only person aboard. He looked about him and saw no one. Yet he continued to hear a heated conversation. At last he noticed three coal-black crows perched on a log floating nearby, chattering noisily about their husbands. And from their conversation it became clear that they wished their unfortunate husbands dead.

They must be witches, thought the boy.

"Are you sure there is nobody here who can hear us talk?" asked one of the crows.

"Certainly I'm sure," replied another. "There's no one aboard."

"Then I can tell you a good way to get rid of our husbands," said the first crow. "On their fourth day at sea, we will turn ourselves

41

into waves and wash them overboard. I will be the first wave, and I'll drown my husband, the captain. You, my dear, will then sweep the first mate over the side of the ship. And the third wave will carry the second mate to the depths of the sea. Ha, ha, ha! And then we'll all be widows!"

So delighted were the crows by their cruel scheme that they hopped, fluttered, pecked and cawed with joy. Then for some reason the first mate's wife again became suspicious:

"Are you absolutely certain that no one is listening?"

"No one, no one," the others assured her.

The boy breathed more easily. For a moment he had feared that he'd been discovered.

"If we plan to get rid of them this way," the captain's wife continued, "we are bound to succeed. Only one thing could stop us. But were it to happen, it would cost us our lives!"

"Tell us, sister, tell us!" the two crows begged.

"I will. But suddenly it seems to me that I can smell someone on the bridge."

"That's quite impossible," the others replied. "Someone has

just forgotten to put the fire out, and that's what you smell. Go ahead and talk."

"Well, then. If for some reason three cords of birch logs were piled on this ship—and, mind you, it would have to be exactly three cords, no more and no less . . . and if one cord were thrown into the water, log by log, when the first wave rushed toward the vessel . . . and then if the second cord were thrown in when the second wave neared the ship . . . and then finally the third cord when the third wave approached . . . well then, we would be finished."

"That is true, sister, then we'd be finished, finished, finished!" screeched the other witches, and into the air they whirled, screaming and cawing, and then disappeared.

Certain that the captain would not believe him were he to describe these eerie and frightening events, the cabin boy wondered how to save his friends from death. At last he hit on a plan. The next morning, when the officers and crew boarded the ship, the captain decided to make one more attempt to persuade the boy to remain a sailor.

Now the clever lad told the captain that he would go along under two conditions. First, he said, three full cords of birchwood had to be placed aboard. And second, on a certain day and at a certain time, he must be permitted to take full command of the ship.

"What?" exclaimed the captain. "A cabin boy in command? Who ever heard of such nonsense?"

But the boy replied that these were his conditions, and he would not sail unless they were met.

"This is most unusual," snapped the captain. "It's ridiculous," snorted the first mate.

"But let's agree to his silly requests," the second mate said with a wink. "Let him think he has command of the ship when he wants it. If anything goes wrong, we can always take over again."

So the captain ordered that three full measures of birch logs be brought aboard. And when the logs were neatly stacked, the vessel set out to sea.

When the fateful fourth day arrived, the ocean was calm and its mirror-smooth surface reflected bright sun and blue skies. "Now I must take command of our ship," the cabin boy announced. "And we must prepare for a storm. The sails must be rolled back and tied to the spars. All hands must be put to work at once." The boy shouted to the crew to reef the sails. The captain and the crew laughed when the command was given, but the boy insisted that his order be obeyed.

"It is clear that our young friend hasn't learned the first thing about seamanship," the captain said to his mate. "But since no harm can come from this, and since I have also given him my word that he will be in command for this one day, we must do as he orders."

"Reef the sails," the boy directed again.

"Reef the sails!" the mates repeated.

No sooner had this been done than a violent squall came up, buffeting the ship so furiously that it would have capsized had not the sails been reefed. Then a giant wave slowly gathered and rolled menacingly toward the ship. As it approached, the boy ordered that the first cord of birchwood be thrown overboard, log by log, one log after the other, and never two logs at a time.

The sailors had long since stopped laughing, and they hastened to obey the boy. They hurled the first cord of wood overboard, log by log. And when the last piece splashed into the water, a terrible groan could be heard. As the haunting howling faded, the winds ceased. The sun glimmered again on smooth seas.

The captain affectionately put his arm on the boy's shoulder. "That was well done, my lad. I am going to make it known far and wide that you saved the ship and our cargo."

"Our troubles are not yet over," replied the boy. "A much stronger storm approaches."

Then he ordered that every loose object be securely fastened to the deck. No sooner had the crew finished its work than the second squall, far more powerful and destructive than the first, rocked the boat. Rain whipped the decks, brutal winds snapped spars; and the terrified crew saw an enormous wave form in the distance and come hurtling toward them. Now the boy ordered that the second cord of birchwood be thrown overboard immediately, log by log, and under no circumstances two logs at a time. And when the last piece of birch fell into the ocean, everyone again heard a deep and horrible groan. And as it faded, the sea became calm.

When the captain turned to the boy to praise and thank him again, the boy simply said, "The worst is yet to come." Then he ordered each sailor to his post.

Now an even more dreadful storm tormented the ship, tossing it and thudding it with crashing waves. And from the distance there rolled toward them a wave as vast as a mountain, a wave that seemed able to swallow the world itself. "Do not be afraid," shouted the cabin boy. "Drop the third cord of birchwood into the sea. Drop it in log by log, and never two pieces at a time! And hurry!" The crew obeyed, and when the last piece slipped below the seething surface, a terrible groan was again heard. Then the waves became ripples, and the black storm clouds changed to white cotton puffs, and the sun warmed the ship with golden rays.

The captain and his mates again congratulated the boy, and with promises of great reward set sail and continued their trip.

When they finally reached Oslo many months later, the captain and the mates expressed the hope that their wives would be waiting for them at the dock.

"Forget your wives," the boy said. "You have no wives."

"What are you raving about?" the captain angrily demanded.

Then at last the boy revealed all that had taken place. But the captain didn't believe him. He rushed ashore and ran to his home. When he found no one there, he sped to the grocer and the butcher to ask after his wife. But none could say where she was. They did however tell him that along with the wives of the first and second mates, she was last seen on a day of strange storms and groaning noises.

The captain immediately returned to his ship, bearing with him a satchel filled with gold—his grateful reward for his cabin boy. And the boy did return to sea. Indeed, a few years later he was the proud captain of his own fine vessel.

The Soria~Moria~Castle

Perhaps the most famous of the traditional Nor-
wegian fairy tales, this is the story of a young man
in search of his enchanted princess. This is adapted
from the Asbjornsen version.

Once upon a time there lived a couple who had a tall, handsome son named Halvor. Unlike other lads his age, who by this time were learning a trade or working at it, Halvor preferred to sit at home by the fireplace, quietly thinking. Even when his parents sent him off to apprenticeships in different towns, Halvor would soon run away and return to his beloved fireplace.

One day a ship's captain visited Halvor's parents. Before returning to the boat, he asked the lad to sail to sea with him and visit many different foreign countries. And to everyone's surprise, Halvor replied that he would like to do nothing better than go to sea.

His mother quickly packed Halvor's bag, and off the lad went. Halvor learned to love the life of a sailor, and each day was long and busy. Then, far out from land, the schooner ran headlong into a hurricane, and was thrown off course. After drifting for several days the boat was driven against a strange coast recognized by nobody on board. And as the wind had completely subsided, they could not set sail, but had to lie off shore. Bored by the total inactivity and attracted by the land, Halvor asked the captain for permission to go ashore. Though at first the captain didn't like the idea, he agreed after Halvor promised to return as soon as the wind picked up.

Halvor rowed ashore, and there before him was the most beautiful country he had ever seen: wide open fields, cherry orchards, pine forests—but nowhere any people. Soon the wind rose, and it was time for him to return to his ship. And yet Halvor felt that he had not seen enough of this strange country. He decided to stay. And once he had made this decision, he began to walk across the great green fields.

46

At last he came to an unusually
wide, white road, so level and mirror-smooth that he could have rolled
an uncooked egg on it without
breaking the shell. He continued
down this road for many hours, but
not until evening came and the sun
set did he notice the huge and magnificent castle in the distance. Halvor hadn't eaten a thing all day, and
by this time he was ravenously hungry. He decided at once to continue
on to the castle, and ask there for
food and shelter.

But the nearer he came to it, the
more menacing the castle appeared,
and Halvor grew fearful. Jagged
cliffs surrounded it, and strange
birds with sharp beaks fluttered
about him. Nevertheless he mus-
tered his courage, crossed the draw-
bridge, and entered the castle by
the main gate. An enormous fire
burned in the hearth of the great
hall; yet no one was there in the vast

room to greet him. He walked further, and came to the kitchen. There he saw large quantities of food cooking on the stove, and on an enormous table—as if in preparation for a feast—were many plates of gold, and sparkling silver goblets. Halvor waited in the kitchen for a while, expecting that cooks or serving-maids or even guests would soon appear; but when no one came he continued his weary walk through the castle. To his surprise room after room was empty. At last when he had just about given up hope of finding anyone, he noticed a gleaming door that was smaller than any of the others, made of solid gold and bedecked with jewels. He opened it. And there Halvor saw a beautiful princess spinning behind a spinning wheel.

"Oh!" she cried out when she saw Halvor, "has a Norwegian really come here? After all these years? Poor young man—I must send you away immediately. Even now it is almost too late. In less than five minutes the troll will return and swallow you up. For this is the castle of the troll with three heads."

"If he had four heads, I wouldn't leave," Halvor replied bravely. "I want to see such a creature. And I am not afraid of him, because I have done nothing wrong. But please give me something to eat first because I am famished."

After he finished eating a supper of roast grouse, the princess said to Halvor, "Do you see that sword hanging on the wall? See if you can swing it around your head." Halvor tried, but the sword was so heavy that he could not even lift it, much less swing it around his head.

"Just as I thought," said the princess. "You must first drink from the flask that hangs beside the sword. The three-headed troll always does so before he uses the sword."

Halvor raised the flask to his lips and sipped the bitter liquid it contained. Now the sword did seem as light as a hummingbird's feather. "Let the troll come!" said Halvor. "Now I'm ready for him." And he hid behind the door.

No sooner said than done. With a deafening roar and rush of wind, in stamped the hideous troll with three heads, hissing and howling.

"Fie!" he bellowed, and his hair stood on end. "I smell Norwegian blood!"

"Indeed you do," Halvor shouted back, and with one mighty swing of the sword he cut off the troll's three heads.

The princess was overjoyed, for now she was free of the evil spell that had condemned her to serve forever as housekeeper to the monstrous troll. But her happiness lasted only a moment; then Halvor saw tears in her eyes. "I have two sisters," she said, "who are also prisoners of trolls. One is in a castle twenty miles away, and the second is locked in a castle about fifty miles distant."

Halvor assured the princess that he would rescue her sisters. Early the next morning, even before the sun had risen, Halvor was on his way. He neither rested nor tarried, but kept walking all day. And as dusk fell he saw in the distance a huge castle, even more magnificent and awe-inspiring than the one he had just left. And though he was again somewhat frightened, Halvor entered without hesitation. Again the vast halls and chambers, even the kitchen, were empty. But he kept walking until he came upon a door made of solid silver. Without knocking he entered, and there before him was a beautiful princess spinning with silver thread.

"A Norwegian!" she gasped. "How amazing that you even dare enter here. I don't know how many hundreds of years I have been imprisoned in this castle, and never in all this time has a human crossed the moat. But as overjoyed as I am to see you, young sir, I must warn you—leave here this very moment. This is the castle of the troll with six heads, and he will devour you if he finds you."

"Even if he had twelve heads," replied Halvor, "I would not leave. But I am hungry and thirsty. Have you food to serve me?"

After he had finished eating a delicious dinner of wild duck, dumplings and red cabbage, the princess again begged Halvor to flee.

"No," he insisted, "I will not depart. I have done nothing wrong and therefore I need not be afraid of anything or anyone."

"In that case," said the princess, "see if you can lift the sword that hangs on the far wall." As vigorously as he strained, Halvor could not raise the weapon. "Then sip from the bottle that stands on the table," directed the princess. And no sooner had the bitter liquid touched his lips than Halvor felt the strength of a giant rising within him. And as he lifted the sword, in charged the troll, each of his heads hissing steam.

"Fie," the troll roared, making the very walls tremble, "I smell a human! He is a worm I am going to swallow whole!"

But Halvor raised the sword and with one swing of the glistening blade sliced off the troll's six heads.

Now Halvor added to the joy of the young princess by telling her that one of her sisters was also newly free, and that he would soon be on his way to rescue the third.

Early the next morning he set forth again. Knowing that this castle was even farther away than either of the previous ones he walked all day without stopping once. At last, near nightfall, he saw the castle looming in the distance. By this time Halvor knew exactly what to expect. He entered through the main gate, then walked through to the kitchen and down the long, lonely corridors. He didn't even try any of the doors until he came to a portal made of platinum. This he swung open and there found a princess beautiful beyond words. She said at once, as had her sisters, that no Norwegian had ever been there before, and next she begged him to leave because the horrible troll with nine heads was due to arrive any minute and would unquestionably devour him.

But Halvor wasn't discouraged. "Even if he had nine times nine heads, I would not leave," he said. "Let the troll come!"

So the princess also gave Halvor a magic sword and told him to sip from the troll's magic flask. No sooner had Halvor put down the flask then the troll whirled in, fuming and shouting, "Fie, fie, fie . . . a thousand times fie . . . I smell Norwegian blood." But Halvor laughed as the gruesome troll approached, and with one swift stroke of the sword he cut off the troll's nine heads.

And then there was a glorious feast. The three princesses celebrated their freedom, happier now than they had ever been before. All three seemed in love with Halvor, and he with them; but the youngest of the three princesses was most in love.

As the banquet progressed, the three princesses noticed that Halvor frowned and grew quiet. And when they asked him why he appeared so unhappy, he told them that he was homesick, and wanted to see his parents again.

"That's easy enough to arrange," the princesses replied. "If you follow our directions you can go home and return unharmed. All you need do is wear this ring. It has the special power of taking you wherever you wish to be.

"But we must warn you that there are two things you must never do. First, never tell our story or even mention our names to anyone. And second, guard this ring carefully. Should you lose it, disaster will overtake us. We will have to go away . . . far, far off, to the Soria-Moria-Castle."

"I promise that I will never do anything you don't want me to do," vowed Halvor.

Then the princesses weaved fine new clothing for him with

their threads of silver, gold and platinum; and Halvor soon looked so very handsome that truly he seemed a prince.

Then he said, "I wish I were at home in my country." And even before he had finished the sentence, the young man stood before his parents' house.

It was late afternoon and his father and mother were returning from their work in the fields. When they saw Halvor, majestic in his gleaming clothes, they didn't recognize their son. Indeed, they thought him a nobleman who had strayed off his route and lost his way. They bowed low, and asked if there were anything they could do for this noble stranger. Halvor merely asked them to give him shelter for the night. At first they politely refused, feeling that their humble home was not fit for so grand a gentleman. But when Halvor insisted that he would be perfectly satisfied just to sit by the fireplace all night, they consented.

Thus Halvor entered his own home, unrecognized by his own parents. He sat down by the hearth, gazing at the glowing coals, quietly thinking, as he had for so many years before.

His parents talked about many things until Halvor asked them if they had any children. With tears in their eyes they told him how their only son had gone to sea and had never been heard of since. Hearing this, Halvor smiled and asked, "Couldn't I be your son?"

"Of course not," his mother cried out. "Halvor was a fine lad, a good son, and smart—but he was lazy, and he would never have amounted to anything. As for his clothes, they were nothing more than rags. Not in his entire life could my dear, sweet Halvor ever earn enough money to be able to dress the way you are dressed."

But when the old woman stepped to the hearth to stir the coals, the light from the bright flames fell on Halvor's face, and at last she recognized him.

"Are you really my son?" she cried out. Then Halvor told them all that had happened since he had left home.

Halvor's mother was so proud of her son that she wanted to show him off to those of her neighbors who in the past had thought him only an idler. When mother and son reached the neighbor's house, Halvor's mother entered first.

"I would like you to see my son, who has just returned from a long voyage. He has made his fortune abroad, and looks just like a prince," she proudly proclaimed.

But her neighbors didn't believe her. They threw their heads back and laughed as if this were the silliest thing they had ever heard. And when the old woman insisted she was telling the truth, one of the young ladies said, "Your Halvor looking like a prince? Stop telling us such silly things, woman! I wager he's the same fellow he always was. Covered with ashes from the fireplace, and dressed in rags . . ."

But she never finished her sentence, because Halvor entered the house at that precise moment. When the girls saw him in his magnificent garb, they were so ashamed that they hung their heads in embarrassment, and dared not even look up.

Halvor was angry and said, "Isn't it time you stopped thinking that there is no one more refined or beautiful than you? You ought to see the princesses I freed from the clutches of the trolls. Compared to any one of them you look like milk-maids. And the youngest princess, who was kept in captivity by the nine-headed troll, is more beautiful than either the sun or the moon. I wish they were here so that you might see them."

Halvor had scarcely uttered these boastful words when the three princesses stood beside him in the room. It was then that he realized he had unthinkingly betrayed their trust, that he had broken his promise never to mention their names or their story to anyone. A feeling of doom overtook him. But the princesses did not utter a word of reproach. They simply stood beside him, smiling and more beautiful than all the stars in the heavens.

When Halvor left with the three princesses they strolled about the countryside until they came to a lake. The youngest princess then said, "Let's all sit down and rest." And as they sat there and stared into the mirror-like surface of the lake, the lovely princess gently stroked Halvor's forehead. Soon he was fast asleep. She slipped the magic ring from his finger and replaced it with an ordinary band. Then she cried out, "Hold on tightly, sisters, and let us be off to the Soria-Moria-Castle!"

And into the night they disappeared, leaving the sleeping Halvor behind.

When he awakened a few hours later, Halvor sensed at once that the three princesses had deserted him. He wept and lamented, and his despair was so grievous that no one could help him. His parents tried to cheer him up, but did not succeed. His mother served him his favorite foods, but Halvor would not eat.

Soon they understood that Halvor would once again have to leave them. And when that day came, the young man gently kissed his parents good-bye and told them that he would probably never return,

52

since he could not live without his princess. And then he set forth, vowing to find his beloved even if it meant going to the end of the world.

At twilight of the first day of his journey, he met a man who led a tired old nag by its bridle. For some inexplicable reason, Halvor felt that he had to own this horse. Greeting the stranger politely, he asked whether he might buy the animal. The man didn't seem at all surprised at Halvor's query, but he warned Halvor that the horse wasn't worth owning, since it would never permit itself to be ridden nor would it ever agree to pull a cart. But this information didn't disturb Halvor at all. He made the stranger a generous offer, and it was accepted without a word. Halvor then took the horse, placed his knapsack on it, and moved on. He led it through a forest, not knowing where he was going. When evening came he lay down under a tree, and though he was willing to let the horse roam about freely, the animal lay down next to Halvor and didn't move from his side. That night Halvor was exhausted; yet he could not fall asleep. Something seemed to be urging him to move on. Thus before long he arose and continued his long trek through the seemingly endless forest. Whenever he came to a clearing he would let his horse run free and graze. But if he himself paused for even a moment, it appeared as if the twigs and branches of the trees had turned into long beckoning arms, motioning him forward.

Thus Halvor wandered through the great forest for three days and three nights, without sleeping. He had no idea where he was or where he was going. There was only the strange inner feeling that persistently urged him on and on and on, making it impossible for him to pause for rest.

On the fourth night, as he stumbled with desperate weariness through the enormous forest, he detected a light glinting through the trees.

"Perhaps people are there," he thought. "Perhaps they will allow me to sit next to their fire and warm myself. And perhaps they will even have something for me to eat."

When he neared the light he saw that it came through the cracked windows of a tiny, broken-down shack. Peering through the window he saw a very old man and a very old woman. Their hair was grey, and their skin was wrinkled; and Halvor noticed that the old woman's nose was so long that she used it as a poker with which to stir up the ashes in the fireplace. Yet so tired and hungry was Halvor that he promptly entered.

"Good evening, good evening," said the old woman. "Pray

tell us what or whom you seek. It is rare that we see a Norwegian in this part of the country. More than a hundred years have passed since the last one passed our door."

"I am looking for the Soria-Moria-Castle. Do you know the way?"

"No," the woman replied, "I do not. But soon the moon will be coming, and I shall ask him. He should know, because he sees and illuminates everything."

And as soon as the moon rose and stood bright and clear above the treetops, the old woman slowly rose from her chair and went outdoors.

"Oh moon," she cried, "oh, old friend moon, can you show me the way to the Soria-Moria-Castle?"

"I am sorry, grandmother, but I cannot help you. For when I sent my silver light in that direction, a cloud came by and blocked my vision."

"The moon doesn't know," said the old woman to Halvor. "But if you can wait a few minutes, the West Wind will arrive, and he will certainly know the way to the castle because he blows everywhere and knows everything about this world."

It was then that the old woman saw the horse. "Why don't you lead the poor beast to the pasture to graze?" she asked. And then she looked at Halvor, and with a hesitant voice she said, "Perhaps you would like to make a trade with me? I have a pair of old boots that will carry you twelve miles with every step you take. They should help you get to the Soria-Moria-Castle much faster. What say you give me the horse for the boots?"

Halvor was pleased to make the exchange and the old woman appeared overjoyed. She began to hobble around and shout, "Now, at last, I can also ride, now I can also ride!"

Then Halvor tried to tell her that the horse could not be ridden. But before he could say this the old woman had clambered up on its back—and the horse didn't seem to mind at all. Instead, he merrily trotted around the house.

Halvor then took the boots and wanted to move on. But the old woman told him to lie down by the hearth and rest, because she felt that he should at least wait until she had talked to the West Wind.

Halvor didn't have to wait long. Suddenly the walls of the hut creaked loudly and the boughs of the trees began to bend. The old woman raised herself from her seat and hobbled outdoors. "Oh West

Wind, oh dear West Wind," she shouted, "can you tell me the way to the Soria-Moria-Castle? A man is here, who must get there."

"Of course I know the way, grandmother," the West Wind replied. "In fact, I'm on my way there now. I have to dry some linens that are hanging on a line. And I must be there before the wedding! Tell your friend that he can come along with me, if he wants to. But he'll have to hurry, because I can't wait."

Hearing this Halvor ran outside.

"I hope you can keep up with me, good man," the West Wind howled. And saying that he was off, whistling over mountains and valleys, over land and water.

Even with his twelve-mile-boots, Halvor could scarcely keep up with the wind. And after about an hour, the West Wind said to Halvor, "I have to leave you now. Before I go to the castle to dry the linen, I must first blow down a section of a forest. But you won't get lost. Just follow the mountains and soon you will come upon some girls washing linen in a clear brook. They will show you the way to the Soria-Moria-Castle."

Halvor thanked the West Wind for his help and continued on alone. Soon he saw the girls; and when they spied Halvor, they didn't say a word, but silently pointed toward the path he had to take.

Halvor had seen many unusual things in the past year. But nothing was more beautiful than the Soria-Moria-Castle. Sitting on the side of a mountain, beneath an eternally blue sky and the brilliant golden sun, was a palace cut from diamonds. Each turret was studded with jewels that glistened in the sun. Surrounding the castle were not the usual moats and walls, but gigantic flowers blooming in bright purples, orange, blue and gold and silver. And on the highest spire sat two eagles, one snow-white and the other velvet-black.

Entering the castle's courtyard, Halvor saw that it was crowded with people dressed in velvet robes. Then he realized how dirty and ragged his own clothes had become during his long journey through wild thorny brush and over rocky cliffs and crags. Ashamed of his appearance, Halvor didn't mingle with the splendidly dressed people.

But when the wedding began, Halvor was invited to take a seat at the banquet table. As was the custom, a toast was offered to the bride and bridegroom, and everybody was asked, nobles and servants alike, to join in this wish for happiness.

When the cup-bearer came to Halvor and filled his glass, he drank to the health of the princess. Then he slipped the false ring, which the princess had given Halvor while he was asleep, into the cup, and asked the cup-bearer to take it to the bride with his greetings and best wishes.

No sooner had the princess received the ring than she rose from her seat and proclaimed, "Who has earned the right above all others to marry one of us? He who freed us from the terrible trolls, or he who sits here next to me?"

When Halvor heard this, he left the room, took off his ragged clothes and dressed himself in the magnificent wedding robes of a prince of the realm. Then he returned to the banquet hall.

When the princess saw him thus attired, she pointed at Halvor and said, "There he is, there is the right one."

The people then chased the false bridegroom away, and Halvor took his place, and married the princess.

Though nobody knows where the Soria-Moria-Castle is, there is no doubt that it exists somewhere in a far-off land where the sun always shines bright and where the friendly West Wind blows. And should you ever get there, you will find a beautiful and happy people ruled by the magnificent prince Halvor and his bride, who, it is said, is more beautiful than either the sun or the moon.

The Clever Little Tailor

*"Brains over brawn" has been a favorite subject of
folklore from the beginning of time. This version
from Switzerland dates from the 17th century.*

witzerland, as you know, is a land of towering mountains,
with peaks that reach high above the clouds. But did you
also know that in olden days there lived in this country, particularly in the forests, giants who possessed incredible
strength?

Once two of these giants met in a forest near Lucerne. So
delighted were they by their new friendship that they wandered together
in search of yet another companion. They walked all day and looked
far and wide, but had no success. Then one of the giants, impatient and
sad and annoyed, angrily picked up a huge boulder and hurled it into
the air. It landed with a crash many miles away; and even while the
echoes were still heard there were new sounds: angry complaints,
shouts and groans. Then they saw a mighty head, topped by brush-thick
hair, rising above the trees. By accident, the rock had hit another giant!
And now he was looking around, trying to find who had thrown the
rock. The two giants greeted the newcomer enthusiastically, for now
they had found their third companion.

But as frequently happens when three strangers meet, an
argument arose. One of the giants wanted to walk toward the east; the
second preferred the north; the third insisted on a southern route. Because they couldn't resolve their differences, they separated, each going
in the direction of his choosing.

But all three giants were now angry, since none enjoyed
walking alone. And as they stamped along, each one vowed that he
would kill the first man he met.

Only a few minutes elapsed before the strongest giant saw a
little tailor coming down the road toward him.

57

"You've arrived just in time, little man," the giant screamed in fury. "Say your prayers, because I'm going to hang you on a tree."

The little tailor was very much afraid when he saw the giant and heard him speak, but outwardly he remained calm and did not betray his fears. "Then come on over here," he shouted back. "I'm not afraid of you. I'm just as strong as you are."

The giant strode to the side of the road, and easily lifted a rock that weighed at least a ton. Then he bade the tailor do the same.

"Ha, I can do much better than that," replied the tailor. "I won't even bother with something as simple as lifting a stone that weighs a ton. *I* can squeeze a flint stone between my fingers. Let's see you do that."

The giant angrily picked up a stone. But no matter how hard he tried, he couldn't squeeze the stone. "You lie," the giant roared. "If I can't do it, you certainly cannot."

The little tailor then bent over and pretended to search for a suitable stone. But instead he reached into his knapsack and pulled out a firm round ball of white cheese. So deftly and quickly did he do this that the giant didn't notice what had taken place; he believed that the tailor had indeed picked up a stone. Then the tailor pressed the ball of cheese in his fingers until water streamed from it.

When the giant saw that, he was flabbergasted; and from that moment on he considered the tailor his equal in strength, and suggested that they travel together.

Soon these unlikely companions came to a city where a king lived in great splendor. But when they arrived, there was only sadness and deep mourning at the palace, because the king's beautiful daughter was to be given to a dragon on that very day. For many years this terrifying monster had plagued the kingdom, and had devoured one of its citizens every day. The desolate king had proclaimed throughout his realm that he would give both his daughter and his kingdom to anyone who killed the dragon. But despite this rich promise, no one dared meet the horrible and dangerous monster in combat.

When the giant and the tailor heard of this reward, they decided to attempt to slay the dragon. "With my brains and his supreme strength," thought the tailor, "we have a good chance."

And so they went to the king and informed him that they intended to fight the dragon, and forever free the kingdom of fear.

The tailor and the giant then made their plan of battle. It was agreed that the giant would be armed with a hammer weighing five hundred pounds, while the tailor would carry an equally heavy pair of tongs. The tailor knew, of course, that he would never be able to lift the

huge tongs from the ground; nor could he confess that he was not really as powerful as the giant, for then his companion might turn on him in fury. And so he asked the giant to walk on ahead without him, carrying both the hammer and tongs, until he had "tied his shoelaces." Thinking that the tailor would soon catch up with him, the giant threw the hammer over his shoulder, tied the tongs to his belt, and began to walk. And since a giant's step is giant-size, he was out of the city and at the dragon's cave when the tailor finally caught up with him.

At the dragon's cave the tailor and the giant again discussed their plan of attack. They agreed that the giant would enter the cave first, and with his hammer drive the dragon into the open. Meanwhile the tailor would be waiting just outside the cave, ready to drop the tongs around the monster's neck the moment it emerged.

Courageously the giant lifted the enormous hammer above his head and entered the cave. The little tailor, however, left the tongs where they were—he couldn't have raised them an inch even if he tried! —and peered into the cave. From it came raging howls, frightening growls, hideous hissing, booming bellows. But the tailor couldn't see a thing in the pitch-black cave. Then suddenly he felt a stream of scalding steam, and before he could jump to one side the dragon shot out of the cave, his nostrils shooting flames and his gaping jaws wide open. With one gulp he swallowed the tailor!

But the giant was not far behind, and with one final blow of his powerful hammer he felled and killed the monster. Then he quickly cut open the dragon's belly—and out jumped the plucky tailor. Furious at the tailor for having contributed nothing to the defeat of the dragon, the giant shook his fist at his little companion. "The king has only me to thank for freeing the city from the evil monster!" he roared.

"What?" screamed the tailor, "just because you pounded the dragon on the head with a hammer, you dare think of yourself as a hero? Don't you know that I deliberately jumped into the dragon, because I wanted to turn him inside out? And I was just about to do so when you stupidly sliced him open! How much better it would have been to enter the city dragging an inside-out dragon."

The giant believed every word that the tailor spoke, and agreed that his companion had just as much right as he to present himself at court as a dragon-killer.

Then they were off to the palace, where they laid the dead dragon at the king's feet. The king, who had every intention of keeping his promise to turn over his kingdom and his daughter to the dragon slayer, was now perplexed. Which of the two had earned the honor of marrying his daughter? It was impossible for his daughter to marry *two* people. And it wasn't feasible for the kingdom to be ruled by two men. The king called on his counselors for advice; they pondered the case for sixty days and sixty nights, but could arrive at no solution.

Then the tailor thought he had the answer. "My lord," he suggested, "I have an idea that I feel will be acceptable to the giant. Let us have an eating contest. Whoever can eat the most rice pudding will win both princess and kingdom."

This idea pleased the giant very much. Rice pudding was his favorite dish, and he was sure that he would easily be able to eat more of it than the tailor.

That same day the eating contest began. Two mountainous plates of rice pudding were placed before the giant and the tailor. The giant, whose huge appetite matched his size, shoveled spoonful after spoonful into his gaping mouth. But he was surprised to see that the tailor was matching him spoon for spoon. As he was finishing his third plate, the giant was beginning to feel full. He opened all the buttons of his vest and unbuckled his belt. The tailor, however, continued eating, showing no sign whatsoever of slowing down. An hour later the giant threw his spoon down in dismay; he was so stuffed with rice pudding that he couldn't even look at his plate any longer. The tailor, however, still gobbled away and asked for yet another helping. When the giant heard this he declared himself defeated.

A few days later the tailor married the king's daughter, and as a wedding gift he was given the entire kingdom. Gratefully he offered the giant an important position in one of the far-away corners of his kingdom. The giant refused. "I'll stay in this city," he grumbled, "until I learn how a little man like you could manage to eat so much pudding!"

Now the tailor was afraid that if the giant ever learned that he'd been tricked all along, he would become infuriated, and would kill the tailor. Therefore the little tailor said that he was ready at last to confess. "I did not eat one bite of food during the sixty days we waited for a decision by the king's counselors," the tailor declared. "And thus I could eat without stopping."

The greedy giant clapped his hands with pleasure. "I'll do the same," said he. "I'll not eat a thing for sixty days, and then I'll eat rice pudding for eight days in a row, without even stopping to sleep. And then I'll find my other friends, the other two giants—and back we'll come to teach you not to trick and cheat." But of course the moment the giant stopped eating he began to waste away . . . and soon he was blown away by a puff of wind.

Now that it was all over, the tailor-king asked his wife if she knew how he had really managed to do away with so much rice pudding. When she shook her head, he told her that he had tied a sack around his neck. And while the giant actually ate the pudding, *he* merely dropped spoonful after spoonful of rice pudding into the sack.

You can be sure that the clever tailor was a kind and clever king. And his people never had to fear monsters or giants throughout his reign.

The Underwater Castle

*A kind but cautious king meets a strange fate in
this enchanting story from County Cork, Ireland.*

little way beyond the town of Cork there is a great lake
where people go in the winter to skate and to have fun. But
the sport above the water is nothing compared to what is
beneath. For at the very bottom of the lake there are buildings and gardens far more beautiful than any that can be seen now.

It all happened this way.

Long before Saxon foot pressed on Irish ground, there lived
a great king called Corc. His palace stood where the lake now is, in a
round green valley about a mile in width. In the middle of the courtyard
was a spring of fair water, so pure and so clear that it was the wonder
of all the world. The king was very proud about having such a great
curiosity within his palace, but he was also worried that the well might
go dry, because huge crowds arrived every day, not just to look at it
but also to drink from it. To protect it, he had a high wall built around
the well. Further, he gave orders that no one was to use the well water.
Whenever he wanted some for himself, he would send his daughter to
get it, for he did not trust his servants with the key to the door of the
wall around the well.

One night the king gave a grand ball, and there were many
great princes present along with numerous lords and nobles. Bonfires,
whose golden flames licked the sky, were built all around the palace.
Sweet music was struck up by a band of musicians, and everyone
laughed and danced and sang with great abandon. Now, it happened
that an exceedingly handsome prince was present at this great ball.
He was tall, dark-haired, and pink-skinned, and his eyes were bright
and as blue as the ocean. All night long he danced with the king's
beautiful daughter, the two of them wheeling about like feathers in the

63

wind. The more they danced, the better the musicians played, and the better they played, the more the couple wanted to dance.

At last the dance was over, and everyone went into the hall for a grand feast of fine roasted meats and fowl, sweetmeats and cakes, and honey, ale, and wine.

"May it please your majesty," said one of the great lords, "there is more abundance here than the heart could wish, both to eat and to drink—except for water."

"Water," cried the king, delighted. "Water you shall have, my lord, and of such delicious quality I challenge all the world to equal it. Daughter," he said, "go fetch some in the special golden vessel."

The king's daughter, embarrassed to be commanded to perform such a menial task before such a grand company, bent her head and blushed. The king, who loved his daughter very deeply, was sorry to have offended her, but still he could not take back his command now that he had made it. To ease the situation and to make the task more pleasant, he proposed that the young and handsome prince accompany her.

"Daughter," said the king, "I don't wonder that you are fearful of going out alone so late at night, but no doubt the young prince seated next to you will be gracious enough to accompany you."

The young prince was delighted with the honor, and, taking the golden vessel in one hand, he took the princess' hand in the other and led her out of the hall.

They entered the palace courtyard, and very carefully the beautiful princess unlocked the door to the well. With great caution she bent over and dipped the golden vessel in the water. Unexpectedly it became so heavy she suddenly lost her balance and fell in. The young prince tried to save her, but the spring water, once freed, rose so quickly that soon the entire courtyard was inundated. In a state of terrible distraction, the young prince sped back to the king to tell him what had happened. Just as he entered the great hall, the water, which had been rising higher and higher, rushed into the palace and in one towering wave covered everything inside it. It rose to such a height that it buried the palace and the entire valley upon which it stood, until finally it formed the present great lake of Cork.

Strangely enough, neither the king nor any of his guests was drowned in the great flood. Both prince and princess were also saved, and they returned to the banquet hall under water the very next evening.

It is said with great authority that, from that day on, the grand entertainment has never ceased. Every night the musicians play, and the guests dance and laugh and sing, and the handsome prince and princess whirl about like feathers in the wind. According to some, the grand ball will go on and on and on forever, until someone has the luck to bring up from the depths the golden vessel which was the original cause of the mischief. No one doubts that the trouble was meant as punishment for the king for having shut up the well so that no one else could use it.

It is suggested that those people who have doubts about this story travel to Cork, for the lake is still there to be seen, just outside of town. The road to Kinsale passes along one side of it. When the waters are low, the tops of the towers and stately buildings may be plainly viewed at the bottom—at least by those who have the necessary good eyesight.

The Fairy

What happens to two sisters—one kind and the other unpleasant and selfish—is told in this famous 17th century French fairy tale by Charles Perrault.

Once there lived a widow who had two daughters: the older was her favorite, and she did nothing all day but nibble and nap and dress in the finest gowns. The younger girl was made to do all the hard work of the household, and twice a day she had to lift a heavy wooden bucket and carry it a mile to the well, there to fetch water.

One day while she was at the well, an old, bent woman hobbled up and begged for a sip of water.

"I will gladly give you some water," replied the girl. She filled the bucket to the top and raised it to the woman's lips, knowing that it would be too heavy for the woman to hold in her frail, shaking hands.

Having quenched her thirst, the woman—who was really a fairy in disguise—said, "You are as good as you are pretty, my dear, and when you reach home you will find that I have given you a present."

When the girl arrived, carrying the water, her mother scolded her. "How dare you stay away for so long a time?" she shouted angrily. "Your sister and I are thirsty!"

"I am really very sorry to be so late," the girl apologized. But as she spoke, an astonishing thing occurred. Her words took shape in the air, shimmering and shining—and then three red roses, three pearls and three sparkling diamonds gently floated toward the floor.

"What's this!" cried her mother. "What happened at the well?"

The surprised girl told her mother what had taken place—and again as she spoke, gleaming diamonds, cream-white pearls and scarlet roses formed in the air and then fell in lovely mounds.

"Ha," said the greedy mother, "if a little drudge like you had

such good fortune, think what will happen when I send your sister to that well."

The next day the older sister left her house, carrying the empty wooden bucket. But she went unwillingly, not at all pleased with the idea of walking such a long distance. When she finally arrived at the well, a beautiful young lady dressed in lovely silks approached and asked her for a drink of water.

"No indeed!" snapped the girl. "Do you think I've walked all this distance just to be your maid?"

"You are not very friendly nor very polite," answered the stranger, who was really the fairy in disguise. "But I shall also give you a present."

The girl rushed home smiling with delight, so pleased with herself that in her haste she even left the bucket behind.

"Quickly—what happened?" her mother asked impatiently when the older daughter rushed through the door.

But as soon as the girl started to speak, her words formed black and ugly shapes which fell, there turning into hopping toads and slithering snakes.

"How awful!" wailed her mother. "Your sister must be to blame for this."

And so both the mother and daughter rushed angrily toward the girl. But at the sight of these two furious women, the young girl ran off into the forest. And when she knew that she had gone so far that they could not find her, she huddled against an old tree and wept bitter tears.

At that very moment the king's son was riding through the forest. And when he heard her sighs and sobs, he walked to her side and asked why she wept.

Now, when she answered, her words were only that—words. For something far more wonderful had happened: the prince and the girl had fallen in love. And before long, as king and queen, they ruled wisely over a happy land.

The Gift of the Mermaid

*Keeping one's word is the moral of this charming
story from Brittany.*

 long time ago, the fisher folk living off the Breton shore used
to see numerous mermaids rising from the waves of the ocean.
These charming creatures which looked like humans had
lovely red cheeks, long blond hair, and enormous blue eyes.
Often, these ladies of the sea were high-spirited and playful.
What they liked to do best was to come ashore on bright, moonlit
nights and to comb their hair, with combs made of pure ebony and
adorned with gold filigree and great jewels. Sometimes they even sang
and danced. But it was not only at night that they made an appearance.
There were times when they swam ashore in bright daylight. Then they
spread beautiful white linens on the sand and heaped them full with
the most precious treasures. There were beautiful pearl necklaces,
diadems set with great diamonds, gold armbands, rings of all kinds,
and piles of precious stones. Though no one is sure, it is generally
believed that they obtained these treasures from the many sunken ships
that are strewn all over the ocean floor. To all appearance, the mermaids were a kind and graceful folk. However their óne outstanding
characteristic was suspicion. As soon as any human came near, they
wrapped up their treasures and disappeared in the waves.

One day two young girls walked along the beach, looking
for shells. All of a sudden, they spied a mermaid sitting on a rock.
Placed in front of her was a pile of treasures of the kind we have just
described. The mermaid was so involved with her jewels that she did
not hear or see the two young children who were tiptoeing toward her.
Quickly they had reached the rock on which she was sitting, and they
appeared before her. To their great surprise, the lovely mermaid did
not grab her treasures and jump into the ocean. Instead she smiled at

them and said in a lovely and sweet voice, "Come a bit nearer. I want to give both of you a present.

Shyly the girls approached and the mermaid, quickly making two bundles of her treasures, handed one to each of them.

"This is my gift," said she. "But make sure not to open it before you are home with your parents."

The two young girls, who were the children of poor fisher folk, could not have been happier. They thanked the generous mermaid for her gifts and promised not to look at them. Then they bade her farewell and started on their way home. From a distance, the pretty mermaid waved good-bye to them and reminded them once more not to open the bundle before the stated time.

When they were halfway home, one of the girls, who was exceedingly nosy and impatient, said to the other, "Why should we wait until we get home? I'd like to see what great treasures the mermaid has given me."

But the second girl replied, "How can we do that? Didn't we promise the kind lady that we would wait till we were home?"

"What can she do to us if we don't do as she asked?" replied the first girl impatiently. "And for that matter, we are much too far away from the beach for her to see what we are doing."

The second girl was not persuaded.

"Do as you like!" she said. "But I will keep my word." Thus it came about that the one girl continued on home while the other stayed behind. She sat down on a rock and immediately began to open her bundle. But no sooner had she opened the knots and spread out the bundle than she let out a scream of disgust. Inside was nothing but a heap of ashes and dirt. In a fury she grabbed the cloth and flung it away. Then she ran after her friend, shouting from a distance, "Throw your bundle away. The mermaid has fooled us. She gave us no treasures but only a collection of junk."

As disappointing as this sounded to the first girl, she still replied, "I shall still keep my word. If it is truly junk that she has given us, there is time enough to throw it away at home."

Once she reached home, she placed her bundle on the table. Her parents and her brother stood around. As she opened it, their eyes were blinded by the sparkling of the jewels and the gold and silver. There was such excitement that no one could say a word. At last the young girl, with tears in her eyes, said in a choking voice, "This is the gift or the kind mermaid."

70

Then she told her family all that had happened and how her friend had lost everything by not keeping her word.

Needless to say, the poor fisher folk never went hungry again. They built a new house, and they bought land and cattle. Even the brothers of the young girl were endowed with good luck. Each time they went to sea fishing, they returned with an exceptionally good catch.

But to remind these folk of their good fortune, it is said that, up to this very day, their offspring have kept a few of the most precious stones that were found in the bundle the mermaid had given to the little girl.

The Raven and the Fox

Aesop's Fables are favorites throughout the world. This verse is based on the adaptation made by the French 17th century poet, La Fontaine.

ld raven had a lunch of cheese,
Sly fox did smell it in the breeze.
The fox looked up and sweetly spoke,
"Oh raven, on your perch of oak,
Your coat is black, your beak is yellow,
If only now your voice were mellow,
You'd be the fairest in these woods."

Old raven, overjoyed by praise,
And sure he earned it in all ways,
Breathed in deep, let out a croak . . .
And down fell luncheon from the oak!

Snatching up this tasty prize,
Sly old fox was very wise.
"To fall for flattery, good bird,
Is vanity, you must have heard,
Which lesson, if you please,
Undoubtedly is worth the cheese."
A bit too late, the raven swore,
The rogue would never cheat him more.

72

The Thief and the Donkey

The illustration for this second fable by Aesop, as adapted by La Fontaine, is by Gustave Doré (1833-1883), the famed French painter, illustrator and sculptor.

 wo thieves, adept in their profession,

Had a stolen donkey in their possession,

And then an argument arose,

That quickly moved from words to blows.

The question? Whether or not to sell.

And while the thieves fought long and well,

Another thief, who chanced to pass

Quietly, quickly rode off with the ass.

A Most Unusual Thief

Corruption among the powerful is one of the most popular of all folklore themes. In this tale from Andorra a simple and resourceful old man teaches the king and his advisers a lesson they will never forget.

In Andorra, a tiny country nestled high in the Pyrenees between France and Spain, many years ago, there once lived an old thief who was known throughout the country as a very clever person—far too clever to be captured. However, one morning he was so careless and overconfident that he was caught stealing some spices from a shopkeeper. With great satisfaction the police brought the thief before an extremely severe judge who fined the old man very heavily. Unable to pay the sum, the thief had to submit instead to a very lengthy jail sentence. When he arrived at the prison he examined with great thoroughness his cell and the building itself, looking for a means of escape. Finding none, he soon gave up the idea of escape and instead decided upon another way of getting out of jail. Early one morning he called for the jailkeeper.

"Yes," the keeper inquired gruffly, "what do you want?"

"Take me before the king," demanded the thief.

"The king!" The jailkeeper threw back his head and gasped with laughter. "Why should the king see *you?*"

The thief ignored the jailkeeper's scorn.

"Tell him I have a gift for him—of extraordinary value."

The jailkeeper, impressed with the old man's seriousness, finally agreed to arrange the interview.

The next afternoon the thief was taken to the royal quarters. There the king sat upon an enormous throne, looking very impressive and stern.

"Well, well, what is it? What do you have for me?" asked the king. "I don't have all day to spend on the likes of you, you know."

Before replying, the thief noted that the prime minister, the secretary of state, the general of the army, and the head jailkeeper were also present.

"Your Majesty," said the thief, "I have come here to present you with a rare and valuable gift."

Slipping his hand into his pocket, he carefully withdrew a tiny box, elegantly wrapped in gold paper with silver ribbons.

The king took the package and swiftly opened it. Examining the contents, his face suddenly flushed red with rage and his voice filled the room with a series of royal bellows.

"What is the meaning of this? How dare you bring me an ordinary plum pit!"

"True," admitted the old thief quietly, "it is a plum pit." Here he paused for emphasis. "But by no means an ordinary one."

"What do you mean by that?" stormed the king.

"He who plants this pit," stated the old man, "will reap nothing but golden plums."

A moment of astonished silence greeted this news.

Finally the king said, "Well, if that's the case, why haven't you planted it yourself?"

"For a very good reason, Your Majesty," answered the thief. "Only people who have never stolen or cheated can reap the benefit. Otherwise, the tree will bear only ordinary plums. That is why," and the old thief smiled in his most winning way, "I have brought

the pit to you. Certainly, Your Majesty has never stolen anything or cheated."

"Alas," declared the king with great regret in his voice—for he was an honest man no matter what other faults he had—"I am afraid I am not the right person."

"What do you mean?" cried the others present.

But the king remained silent, remembering how he had once stolen some pennies from his mother's purse when he was a little boy.

"Well, how about the prime minister?" suggested the thief. "Perhaps he—"

But the old thief got no further with his sentence.

"Impossible!" blustered the prime minister with a very red face. He had often accepted bribes from people who wanted fine positions in the government. Surely, the pit would never work for him.

"You then, General?" asked the thief, turning to the head of the army.

"No, no," muttered the general with lowered eyes. He had become an enormously rich man by cheating his soldiers of part of their pay.

"Well then, Mr. Secretary of State?" offered the thief.

"I'm afraid not," sputtered the honorable old man, whose conscience was obviously troubling him. Like the prime minister, he had at times accepted money in return for favors.

"Then the head jailkeeper must be our man," said the thief solemnly as he turned to the last candidate.

Silently the jailkeeper shook his head and shrugged his shoulders. "I'm afraid I'm not right either," he said at last. He was remembering how he was always treating new prisoners, sending those who gave him money to the best quarters and reserving the worst cells for the poor and unfortunate.

Refusing to give up, the thief suggested several other officials. Each of the fine gentlemen, however, rejected in his turn the offer of the plum pit that would bear him golden fruit forever.

When the room was entirely still, each official trying to hide his embarrassment, the old thief suddenly burst out laughing.

"You gentlemen," he exclaimed, "you embezzle and you steal, and yet you never end up in jail!" He searched their faces earnestly, and then in a quiet voice, he added, "I have done nothing more than steal some spices, and for this I have been condemned to serve five years in jail."

For quite some time the king and his officials remained silent with shame.

At last the king stirred.

"I would suggest," he said in a low voice, looking at each of his ministers one by one, "that we all contribute to this man's fine, so that he will not go back to jail."

Immediately the necessary money was gathered and placed at the monarch's feet. Calling the old thief to him, the king gave him the money.

"Go, my good man," he said. "You are free. You have spent enough time in prison. From your experience you have instructed us wisely. Ministers and kings sometimes forget themselves. We will remember your lesson well."

And so, with nothing more than a plum pit to help him, the very clever old thief left jail a free man.

The Strangest Thing in the World

Fantasy and magic are the ingredients of this fairy tale with a surprise ending. Although it comes from Spain, earlier Moorish overtones are clearly present.

ow, little one, I will tell you a little story. Ever so long ago there lived a king who had three sons. And it so happened that all three sons fell deeply in love with one princess, a shy, sweet and lovely girl whose parents ruled a neighboring kingdom. But since it isn't possible for three young men to marry one maiden, the sons agreed amongst themselves that their father should decide which would wed the beautiful princess.

"Well, well, well," the old king mused. "This is indeed a difficult problem. I love all of you equally, my sons, and I certainly don't want to hurt any of you, or favor one of you. And so we'll have to invent a contest of some sort." And silently, the king thought, thought and thought.

At long last he smiled. "I direct all three of you," he said, "to go into the world and secure the strangest object you see. The one who returns bearing the most unusual article will be the prince to marry the princess."

The brothers welcomed this proposal, and immediately set forth to search for the strangest thing in the world. Across the fields they walked, arm in arm, and when they came to a crossroad each one went off in a different direction.

The road the oldest brother chose led him to a large city, and there he searched on every street and in every shop, but he couldn't find anything he considered truly unusual. Oh, there were dancing dolls and intricate music boxes and rare jewels—but nothing that could not be found elsewhere. He was quite ready to go on to another town, when he noticed a black-robed rug merchant who had spread a few rugs on the sidewalk. The rug-dealer beckoned him, and halfheartedly the prince approached.

"Well, what do you think of this carpet?" the dealer asked, pointing to a worn, shabby rug.

"It's ugly and it's worthless."

"Ah, but you couldn't be more wrong," the merchant cackled. "This is a magic rug. If you step on it and tell it where you wish to be, there it will take you within the wink of an eye."

"You are a teller of stories," the prince replied.

"Of true stories only! Come—I will show you. Do you wish to be in Madrid? Or on the island of Majorca? Where shall we go?"

"Listen, merchant," answered the prince. "If we can simply fly to the gates of this city, that would be miracle enough."

Poof! They were there. Quickly the prince paid the rug-dealer the five thousand *pesos* he demanded. He did so happily, too, for he was certain that neither of his brothers could possibly find any object so unusual.

*   *   *

The second brother had in the meantime arrived in a small village. There he met a merchant carrying a telescope that was ten feet long.

"My good man," the prince said, "I am looking for something unique—something not to be found elsewhere. What is it that you are selling?"

"I reply to your question with another question," whispered the merchant. "What in this world would you like to see?"

"My older brother," answered the prince.

"Then look through this telescope and tell me whom you see."

The prince did as he was told—and to his astonishment he saw his brother in a far-off city, buying a carpet.

"This is indeed a wondrous device," he gasped. "I must have it!" And the prince paid the merchant the five thousand *pesos* demanded for the telescope. Carrying it on his shoulder, whistling happily, he started home, convinced that neither of his brothers could possibly have found an object more unusual.

The third of the king's sons didn't even reach a village or city. As he trudged along the road, he came upon an old woman selling apples. The prince was hungry, but the apples were wrinkled and wormy. "Good woman," said he, "please find your finest, reddest apple for me." Carefully the old woman searched her basket, and selected from the very bottom an apple so ruby-red that it glowed and glimmered.

"How much do you want for the apple?" asked the prince.

"Five thousand *pesos*," wheezed the old woman.

"I have no time for foolishness," the prince snapped.

"Nor do I! Can't you see that this is no ordinary apple?"

"What's so special about it?" pressed the prince.

"If you touch this apple to the face of a sick person, it will restore him to health again," the old woman said. "And the apple will not spoil for three years."

"Ha!" snorted the prince. "Do you expect me to believe that silly tale?"

Without another word, the old woman led the lad to the side of the road, where an old and crippled man sat moaning. Silently she touched the apple to the sick man's face. Instantly he leaped to his feet, agile and healed.

"This is in truth a wonderful apple," marveled the young prince. "I give you your five thousand *pesos,* and more!" Then he tenderly placed the apple in his pocket, turned, and hurried back to the crossroads, for there the three brothers had agreed to meet.

When all were together again they showed each other the strange objects they had found. And each thought his own the most unusual.

Then the youngest of the king's three sons said, "Let me borrow your telescope, brother. I want to see what the princess is doing." He lifted the instrument to his eyes. And no sooner had he done so than his faced paled and his fingers trembled. "Dear brothers," he said, "I fear that tragedy awaits us. Our dear princess is deathly ill." The brother with the magic carpet bade them step upon it; in the wink of an eye they were at her bedside. The youngest brother then gently touched the apple to her face; and immediately she arose, her illness cured.

Now the young princes went proudly to their father, the king. They showed him the three objects and explained how the life of their beloved princess had been saved.

"Father, I think the princess should be mine," said the youngest. "Without my apple, the princess would never have become well."

But the second son said, "What you say is true. Yet if it hadn't been for my telescope, we would never have known she was ill."

"You are both right, my brothers," said the oldest. "But don't forget that it was my carpet that brought us here in time to save the princess. Therefore I think I should have her for my wife."

The father listened to his three sons, and then said, "It is difficult to choose. But in my opinion, the telescope is the most unusual of these objects. Therefore my middle son deserves the princess."

Since the three sons had agreed to abide by their father's decision, they didn't say another word.

The princess was then brought to the king's palace, and was told all that had taken place. She listened pensively, and then said, "It seems to me, great king, that the greatest merit belongs to your youngest son, who cured me with the apple. I dare say this only because I have always loved him, and because he is the one I desire for a husband."

That, of course, settled the question. The youngest son and the princess were married. The other brothers went out into the world and soon returned with princesses of their own.

But the old king couldn't help wondering why the princess had never before said she loved the youngest prince. Because if she had, he would never have given his sons the difficult task of finding the strangest object in the world.

But then again, little one, there would never have been this little story to tell!

The Bell of Monte Pino

A magical fairy tale, set in the sun-swept heart of Italy. This version dates from the 18th century.

Have you ever been to Pino? It is a pretty town in the center of a plain, and there is a mountain about a mile away. If you climb Monte Pino and look down on the town, you seem to be gazing at a field of bright summer daisies, for all of the houses are painted white and are sparkling clean, and the roofs are daisy-yellow.

A few hundred years ago, people did not climb that mountain. It was bare and ugly, and no plants or flowers grew on its slopes. But, oddly enough, there was one great, tall pine tree standing on the peak of the mountain. It was not an ordinary pine tree—somewhere in it there was a huge, invisible bell that rang day and night, clanging so loudly that all of the people in Pino had become deaf. And the poor villagers had discovered that no one who risked climbing the cliffs of the mountain to try to solve the mystery ever returned. And so they had all decided that it was better to stay deaf than to risk whatever horrible fate overtook the people who went up the strange mountain.

Then one day a wandering violinist named Vincenzo came to Pino. He was a handsome young man and he played his violin beautifully. He walked directly to the main square in the center of the village, and began to play. Soon, he thought, everyone in town would come running toward him, gathering about to hear his music, for this is what happened everywhere he played. But in Pino no one appeared in the doorways or windows, and even the people who strolled about the square walked past with hardly a glance.

Vincenzo was most unhappy when no one seemed to appreciate his fine music. Then he grew angry. *I suppose,* he thought, *that these silly people prefer the gloomy sound of that bell that's been ringing in my ears ever since I came here. Well, I certainly won't be able to earn a living here. I'll just have some lunch and leave this ridiculous vil-*

lage as soon as I've finished eating. He carefully put his violin into its leather case and walked to the nearest inn.

The innkeeper came to take his order.

"Innkeeper, bring me some food. And please hurry—I'm so hungry I could eat hay," said the young musician.

"Yes, it is a beautiful day," his host replied. "You came for a room?"

"No, no," Vincenzo said. "I only want something to eat, sir, and I beg you to get it as quickly as you can. All day I've had nothing but a crust of bread."

"I'm sorry, sir, but we really don't have even a rusty bed," replied the host. "You'll have to find lodging elsewhere."

The violinist was quite puzzled by the conversation. "Sir," he said, "I told you I wanted only food—and I never mentioned quarters!"

"Oh, do you want me to give your horse some water? Gladly, sir. Where is he?"

Vincenzo was thoroughly annoyed. "Are you *deaf?*" he shouted.

"A little," the innkeeper answered.

Now that Vincenzo understood the situation, he used sign language to let his host know what he wanted. Soon a magnificent array of foods was set before him. As the violinist ate, the innkeeper explained that the entire population of the village had been deafened by the bells on the strange mountain. And he also told Vincenzo of the men who had climbed its slopes and had never returned.

When Vincenzo finished his meal he said, "I think I will climb your mountain. This mystery fascinates me." Then he took out his violin and began to polish it.

The innkeeper looked at Vincenzo in amazement. He told him terrible stories that all the townspeople knew—stories about giants and monsters who lived on the cliffs. But Vincenzo would not change his mind. "I'm alone in the world," he shouted, roaring his words into the innkeeper's ear. "There's no one who would be saddened if I did not return, so don't worry about that part of it. And," he added, pointing to his violin, "when I have this friend with me, I fear nothing."

Again the innkeeper looked at the musician in amazement. Because he was deaf, he thought of the violin as only a worthless piece of wood, and he could not understand how anyone could call such a thing a "friend."

And he also did not know that this was no ordinary violin. Vincenzo had not gotten it in an ordinary way.

The violinist had been born into a very poor peasant household. Both of his parents had to work away from home all day, and as a little boy he was quite used to being left alone. While still very young he learned to entertain himself by playing melodies on flutes that he carved out of reeds. He showed a great talent for music, and indeed he always dreamed of owning a violin, but his family was so poor that the child never really expected this dream to come true.

Then one night he dreamed that he was playing a golden violin. When he awakened, he found a beautiful violin at the foot of his bed. He knew that a fairy must have visited him while he was sleeping . . . that she must have left it there. He had never been so happy. And then a terrible thought occurred to him. He knew that if his parents found the violin, they would want to sell it, for they needed the money very badly.

While Vincenzo was trying to think of a way to hide his treasure he heard a tap at the window. He slipped the violin under the sheets and ran to see who rapped. How surprised he was to see his visitor! She was a girl as beautiful as the sun, dressed in a blue silk gown all studded with stars. The girl lifted a finger to her lips, motioning Vincenzo to be quiet, and whispered, "If you don't want anyone to see your violin, just place it upside down on the ground or on the floor. That way it will be invisible to everyone but you." And the girl smiled so sweetly at Vincenzo that he blushed and lowered his eyes. He was trying to mumble a word of thanks when he felt a hand touch his face. He looked up, but the girl had vanished.

As soon as he had recovered from the surprise of the lovely girl's visit, he tried to play his violin. He had hardly touched the bow to the strings when the loveliest melodies he had ever heard came forth. He knew that with this instrument he would always be able to earn his way as a musician.

His father and mother often tried to find the violin, but what the girl had told him was true. All Vincenzo had to do was to place it upside down, and it immediately became invisible to everyone but himself. Vincenzo thought about the girl frequently, wondering if he would ever see her again.

Many years later, when Vincenzo was fourteen years old, he

decided to leave home and earn his own living. He hoped that if he traveled all over the world he would be able to find the lovely girl, for he longed to see her again. He wandered on foot from town to town, from country to country, but he never saw her. And by the time he reached Pino, he had nearly lost hope of ever meeting her again.

The innkeeper's story had a strange effect on Vincenzo. Though he could see no connection between the madly ringing bells and the beautiful fairy, he felt destined to climb the mountain and investigate the curse that plagued the town.

Vincenzo began his climb up the rocky slope. Nothing out of the ordinary happened until he was more than halfway up the mountain. Then he heard a heavy tramping sound, and turned to see a pack of bears loping toward him, growling and snarling fiercely. When he tried to run, Vincenzo found that he couldn't move—some invisible force was holding him.

The bears were close now, and Vincenzo was sure there was no way to escape. Then he heard a soft and sweetly familiar voice whisper, "Music, Vincenzo, music!" Quickly he raised his violin and began to play. When the first lovely strains of music flowed out of the violin, the bears stopped in their tracks as though enchanted; and almost immediately they turned and silently disappeared.

Vincenzo continued climbing the steep slope. He had nearly reached the plateau at the top of the mountain when he saw a huge cloud of fire blocking his path. Unafraid now, he walked up to it, playing his violin. The cloud separated and a path lay before him.

After he had walked across the path through the cloud of fire he saw a gigantic golden monster, laughing wildly. The monster shouted hoarsely, "Come near, violinist, come here."

"Now I am really lost," Vincenzo thought. But he kept playing, and just as he stepped within the monster's grasp, there was a deafening roar and a bolt of lightning struck the monster. Vincenzo watched, bewildered, as the strange beast dissolved and melted into liquid gold.

How beautiful Monte Pino was at that moment! The sun reflected on the melted gold that had flowed into the cracks and crevices in the rock, and the mountain looked like a golden mirror.

There were only a few steps left to the top. Vincenzo quickened his pace. Finally he reached the enormous pine tree, looming forbiddingly in the middle of the vast plateau. An iron bar was nailed to the trunk of the tree and from it hung a huge bell, clanging deafeningly. Vincenzo saw that a tremendous serpent, its tail wrapped around the tree, was pulling the bell rope.

What an ugly beast, Vincenzo thought. *So it is this snake that deafens the kind people of the village. Now I have met the curse of Monte Pino.* He picked up the largest rock he could find and hurled it at the serpent.

When the rock hit the snake there was again a crash of thunder, followed by a violent burst of lightning. The light was so brilliant that for a moment Vincenzo could see nothing.

When he recovered his sight at last, he found that he was standing in the middle of a magnificent room. And before him was the beautiful girl he had been seeking for so long, and whom he loved with all his heart. The girl laughed at the look of astonishment on Vincenzo's face. She held out her hand to him and said, "I am Rosena, the fairy who protected you when you were young, and who helped you by bringing you your violin."

Vincenzo stared. He could only repeat, bewildered, "A fairy?"

"Yes, my dear Vincenzo. I was destined to be your bride from the moment you were born, and that was the reason my good aunt allowed me to help you. But even though my aunt had forbidden it, I liked you so very much that I caressed you."

Remembering the touch of her hand on his face, Vincenzo felt his heart leap.

"My aunt," she continued, "found out that I had disobeyed her. If one fairy breaks a rule, all fairies are endangered. She had to punish me. When I returned to the castle and went to pull the bell rope—for this had always been my special task—she changed me into a serpent, and made the castle disappear under the mountain. The pine tree that remained at the top is really the bell tower of the castle. My aunt told me that I would remain a serpent until someone climbed the mountain and struck me with a stone, as you just did.

"Now the curse of Monte Pino is broken. The castle has returned to the light of the sun. And, if you wish," she added shyly, "we can be married now."

Vincenzo knew that the strange story Rosena told him was true, and that he had come to the end of his wanderings. He and Rosena were wed soon afterward, and they lived happily and contentedly together.

And in the village of Pino there were no more deaf people. No bells ever rang from the castle on the top of Monte Pino, and the only sounds the people of the town ever heard from there was the music Vincenzo played for them, once a week, when they all gathered at the foot of the mountain to listen to the beautiful melodies that came from his violin.

Catherine and Her Fate

"No one can escape his Fate" is a saying and a belief as ancient as Man: This strange folk tale from Sicily proves the point. The author is unknown.

here was once a merchant who was known to be one of the kindest men in his city. He was not a wealthy man, but if people were hungry he would give them food, and if they were cold he would give them lodging.

The merchant had a beautiful daughter named Catherine.

She was still young, but it was easy to see that she was just as good and kind as her father, always ready to share her food and clothes and playthings, for it hurt her to see anyone who did not have as much as she. On holidays she decorated the homes of the poor and the aged with garlands of flowers; and all year long she made their homes beautiful with her kind spirit.

The merchant had never had any special luck in his business. He earned enough to keep him and his daughter living simply but comfortably, and each year he profited just as much from his work as he had the previous year. And he did not yearn for more.

The year that Catherine was fourteen, his luck changed. Every transaction brought in double the amount of money he had expected. At the end of the year, he was a fairly wealthy man, and people said that no one deserved this fine fortune so much as he. And his good luck stayed with him. For the next few years, everything he did seemed to be the smartest, most profitable thing that could be done.

But as the merchant grew richer during those years, he spent less and less time helping other people. It seemed that the wealthier he grew, the harder his heart became. And Catherine, too, began to care more about gowns and new jewels than anything else. More and more often she would say to people who came to her for help, "I haven't time to discuss it." The truth was that she had more time than ever, for now she had many servants to wait on her. Unfortunately, Catherine was becoming lazy and proud.

Soon the merchant was so wealthy that he had more treasures than even the king. In the largest hall of his great mansion he placed three chairs, one made of silver, the second of gold, and the third of rare woods studded with diamonds. And when he was not making money, he tried to think of a fourth and yet more magnificent chair for the hall.

One day Catherine was sitting idly in her room when suddenly the door opened and a tall, beautiful lady appeared. In her hands she held an exquisitely carved ebony wheel.

"Catherine," the lady asked, "when would you prefer your life to be pleasant and easy? While you are young or when you become old?"

It was a difficult question, and Catherine thought about it for a long time. Finally she replied, "When I am old."

"It will happen as you have wished," said the beautiful lady. She twisted the wheel and watched it spin freely around. When it stopped, she disappeared.

Catherine did not know then that the lovely lady was her Fate, and could control her life.

A week later, Catherine's father learned that his largest merchant ship had sunk in a heavy storm. Another week had not passed before he was informed that several more of his ships had been wrecked in another storm. From then on, every business agreement the merchant made collapsed for one reason or another. For some inexplicable reason, luck had suddenly turned against him. Six months after the strange lady had visited Catherine, the merchant didn't have a penny to his name. The chagrin of having lost so great a fortune was too much for the old man, who became very ill and soon died. Catherine was now all alone in the big house, and she decided to pack her few belongings, move to another city, and try to find a job.

She had just arrived in the new city and was walking along the strange new streets, a little frightened, when she met a lady who asked her where she was going.

"Oh, dear lady," Catherine replied, "I am new to your city, and I am very poor. Could you, by any chance, employ me as a servant?"

It happened that the lady had been looking for someone to help around the house, and so Catherine was hired.

Two weeks after Catherine had started working, her mistress said, "Catherine, I must go on a short trip. I am leaving the house in your care while I am away."

Almost immediately after her mistress left the house, the door opened and Catherine's Fate entered. She wore a long green satin dress and in her hand she held the ebony wheel.

"Catherine," she said, "you didn't think that I was going to leave you in peace, did you? For I cannot do that now."

Then Fate opened a closet, took out the entire wardrobe owned by Catherine's mistress, and began to rip every one of the dresses and coats and hats she had found. Catherine begged her to stop, but her Fate ignored her and calmly continued to destroy the clothes. Weeping bitterly, Catherine fled the house in terror, thinking that her mistress would certainly have her jailed when she found all her clothes ruined. As soon as Catherine had left, Fate turned her ebony wheel, and all the clothes were magically repaired and returned to the closet.

Catherine ran until she was well outside the city, but she did not feel safe until she found herself on the streets of yet another city. Again she was walking through the streets when she met a lady who asked where she was going. And when Catherine said that she was looking for a job, she was quickly hired. But again, on the very first night that her mistress left her alone in the house, Catherine's Fate appeared and destroyed her employer's complete wardrobe.

"You didn't really think that you could escape from me, did you, Catherine?" the lady asked in a soft voice. But Catherine, terrified, hardly heard her Fate's words, for she was already running toward the door.

For seven sad years Catherine's Fate pursued her. Catherine ran from one city to another, but she could never escape her Fate.

At the end of these seven years, Catherine had settled in a new town and had again met a lady who wanted to employ her. The lady warned Catherine, however, that she would have to perform one daily chore that was strange and difficult.

"You need only tell me what it is," Catherine said, "and if I can possibly manage it, I will do it happily."

"Do you see that high mountain over there?" the lady asked. "Every morning you will have to carry a large plate of freshly baked bread to its summit. And when you reach the top you will have to shout very loudly and clearly, 'Fate of my mistress, Fate of my mistress, Fate of my mistress.' When you have shouted it three times, my Fate will appear and will take the bread from you."

"I will gladly perform that task," Catherine said.

After she had worked at her new job for a few months, her mistress, who noticed that Catherine cried very often, asked her why she was so sad. Catherine told her mistress everything that had happened since her father's death.

"I have an idea," the lady said. "Tomorrow morning when you take the bread to my Fate, why don't you tell her your story and ask her to implore your Fate to leave you in peace now."

The next morning Catherine did as her mistress had suggested. "My dear child," the Fate replied, "your Fate is sleeping beneath seven blankets now, and I do not think it will be possible to disturb her."

After Catherine left, the Fate of her mistress thought about Catherine's story, for it had touched her deeply. Finally she decided to try to arouse Catherine's Fate, and she went to visit her. "Dear sister," she said, "why don't you let poor Catherine regain her happiness? Hasn't she suffered enough?" Catherine's Fate smiled, and replied, "Bring Catherine to me tomorrow morning. I will give her a present."

When Catherine went to the mountain top the following morning, she was taken to her own Fate. And Catherine saw that her Fate was no longer holding the carved ebony wheel, which was now lying near the foot of the bed. As Catherine approached the bed her Fate opened her eyes and said, "You have suffered enough, dear child. Take this piece of silk and guard it well. It will bring you good fortune."

Filled with happiness, Catherine returned to her mistress and related everything that had taken place; but neither of them could guess what possible good could come from a piece of silk.

Soon afterward, it was announced throughout the land that the young king planned to marry. But when the tailor made the king's wedding gown he found that he did not have enough silk. For some reason, no matching material could be found anywhere. The king let it be known that if any of his subjects owned silk of that particular color, he should bring it to the royal court at once.

Catherine's mistress told her that the silk her Fate had given her matched the king's exactly. "Go to the palace, Catherine," she said, "and make the king a gift of your piece of cloth."

Catherine put on her finest dress and went to the royal court. She looked so beautiful that no one at the court—including the king—could take his eyes off her.

"My king," Catherine said, "I have brought you the piece of silk you seek."

"Very good," the king replied. "I will pay you its weight in gold."

A scale was brought to the throne room. On one side the silk was placed, and on the other a piece of gold. But a strange thing happened. No matter how many pieces of gold the king put on the scale, the side containing the silk was always heavier. At last the king placed all his treasures on one side and the piece of silk on the other. But still the scale didn't move. The piece of silk weighed more than all of the king's treasures! The king then took off his crown and placed it on top of the coins and treasures. And the scale moved slowly. When it reached perfect balance, so that the gold, and all the king's treasures, and his crown, weighed just as much as the piece of silk, the scale stopped.

"Where did you get the silk?" the king asked Catherine.

"My mistress gave it to me," she replied.

"No," said the king, "that's impossible, for this is not ordinary cloth. I command you to tell me the truth."

So Catherine told the king the story of her life.

At the court there lived a very wise old woman. When she heard what Catherine had said, she addressed the king. "My sovereign and noble lord," she said, "Catherine must become your queen. That is the way it has been willed, and that is why your crown exactly balanced the scale."

The king had been enchanted by the beautiful Catherine, and he joyously agreed. He sent a message to the princess to whom he was betrothed, telling her that Fate had destined Catherine to become his queen.

And so were they married, and lived happily and ruled wisely till the end of their days.

The Truthful Peasant

All over the world, honesty is considered an outstanding attribute. How a simple man, caught in a dilemma, deals with his conscience is the basis of this folk tale from Sicily. The author is unknown.

here once was a king who owned a goat, a lamb, a ram and a sheep. These were fine animals, the strongest and healthiest in the land, and the king wanted them cared for by someone he trusted completely. Now in this kingdom there also lived a peasant known as 'the truthful peasant,' because he never ever told a lie. The king decided that he was the man to tend his animals. And it was agreed that every Sunday evening the peasant would visit the palace and report to the king on their health.

For many months all went well. The peasant would arrive at the palace, remove his woolen cap, bow low, and say,

"Good evening, your majesty."

"Good evening, truthful peasant. How is my goat getting on?"

"He is white and healthy," the peasant would reply.

"And how is the lamb?" the king would ask next.

"Also white and beautiful."

"And my ram?"

"Fine to look at."

"What news of the sheep?"

"She is beautiful to see."

When they had thus spoken, the peasant would put his cap back on his head, bow again, and return to his farm in the mountain.

But among the officials of the king there was one who envied the regard and respect his majesty accorded the simple peasant. One day this official went to the king and said, "Do you really believe, sire, that your old peasant has never told a lie? I am willing to wager that he will lie to you next Sunday."

"You could not be more wrong," replied the king. "And to

93

show you my absolute confidence in the peasant's honesty, I am ready to lose my head if he lies next Sunday."

The doubter and the king then agreed that whoever lost the bet on Sunday would forfeit his head.

The official now tried desperately to think of some way to

tempt the peasant to tell a lie. But the more he thought about it, the more he realized how difficult a task it was. When only two days remained for him to find a solution, his wife noticed her husband's despair. He explained his problem. "Ha," she answered, "do not give the matter another thought. I know how to handle that truthful peasant."

The next morning she dressed in her most beautiful clothes. Her gown was as white as new snow. Her golden hair fell gently to her shoulders. She wore no jewelry or gems other than a diamond circlet on her forehead. She seemed to be either an angel or a sweet and kindly queen. Then she seated herself in her carriage and set out for the mountain farm where the truthful peasant tended the king's animals. When she appeared before him, the peasant's eyes widened with admiration. Never had he seen so beautiful a woman.

"Good man," she said to him, "would you do me a favor?"

"Noble lady," the peasant replied, "I will help you in any way I can."

"I am ill," she said softly. "And I will recover only if I can eat the roasted liver of a fine sheep. If you do not give it to me, I am afraid that I shall die."

"Dearest lady," replied the peasant in distress, "ask for anything but that. You see, these animals are not mine. They belong to the king. I am only their keeper. Therefore I can't possibly kill them."

"Oh," the lady lamented, "then I shall die, and you might have saved me. Alas, alas! Dear peasant, could you not kill the sheep, and tell the king that the animal died falling down the mountain?"

"No," the peasant replied. "That I certainly could not do."

But the woman continued to plead, and the peasant's sympathy was stirred so profoundly that at last he killed the sheep, roasted its liver, and gave it to his visitor to eat.

"You have saved me," she assured him. "Be certain that I shall be forever grateful." And with these words, the scheming wife of the official departed.

Now the poor peasant was alone with his torment and doubts. What could he say to the king? In his anxiety he took his walking stick, planted it in the earth, and hung his coat on it. Next he stepped back a little way, removed his woolen cap, and then approached it respectfully. Bowing low, he said, "Good evening, your majesty." Pretending first to be the king, and then answering as he would at court on the following night, he continued: "Good evening, truthful peasant. How is my goat getting on?" And as always he replied: "He is white and healthy." But when he came to that point in the conversation when the king would ask, "How goes it with the sheep?" he could not bring himself to answer. He tried to utter a lie: "The sheep has been stolen." He attempted to say, "It has fallen down the mountain." But the lies stuck in his throat. He couldn't speak.

That night, you may be sure, the peasant did not sleep. But by sunrise he had found an answer. Yes, he thought, yes, that will do. He grasped his stick and coat and walked towards the city.

When he reached the castle, he found the king, surrounded by his entire court, sitting in the throne-room.

The peasant removed his cap, and began his report in the customary way.

"Good evening, your majesty."

"Good evening, truthful peasant. How is my goat?"

"He is white and healthy."

"And how is the lamb?"

"Also white and beautiful."

"And my ram?"

"Fine to look at."

"What news of the sheep?"

"My lord and king, I cannot lie, so I must tell you a sad story. The other day there appeared on the high mountain a beautiful lady with a star on her forehead, and feeling sorry for her strange plight, I broke the neck of the sheep—"

"Say no more, my good peasant," interrupted the king. And all present cheered and applauded—except, of course, the official and his wife. They were exiled from the kingdom. The peasant, however, was richly rewarded by the king, and for all the days of his life he remained truthful at all times.

The Czar's General and the Clever Peasant

*Wit and common sense enable the humble man to
defeat the powerful tyrant in this typical folk tale
from Lithuania. The author is unknown.*

 peasant was digging in his garden one day when his spade
unexpectedly hit a hard object. It wasn't a stone and it wasn't
a root. And so he continued to dig around it. And soon he
saw that he had uncovered a metal chest.

It was filled with gold pieces. But what was a poor peasant
to do with so great a fortune? He realized that it was hopeless for him
to try to keep it. He would only be accused of thievery, or the czar's
evil officers would steal it from him. After pondering his problem, he
decided that it would be wisest to take the chest of gold to the czar
himself.

So the peasant dressed in his cleanest clothes, and walked to
the czar's majestic castle. There, in front of the czar's chambers, he was
halted by a haughty general who glared disdainfully at the peasant and
asked, "What do you want, stupid peasant?"

"I have found a chest of gold," was the reply. "I have brought
it here to give it to the czar."

When the general heard the word gold, his eyes gleamed.

"If you agree to give me half the reward the czar gives you,
I will let you enter," declared the general. "But if you refuse my generous offer, I'll have you beaten and thrown into jail this minute."

"You are indeed generous, sire," the peasant replied. "I will
gladly give you half my reward."

So the general went to the czar and announced that a peasant
waited outside, and wished to have a word with his ruler.

"Well, little farmer, what would you like?" the czar asked when the peasant was brought before him.

"Nothing, father czar. I have come only to bring you a gift."

And he opened the lid of the metal chest.

"And what would you like in return for this gift of gold?" the czar inquired.

"Father czar, just give me a hundred lashes of the whip."

"What?" the astonished czar exclaimed. "You ask for a hundred lashes? You have brought me gold and you want a hundred lashes? No, no, no; you certainly deserve better."

"Please, father czar," the peasant insisted. "I don't want any other reward. Just give me a hundred lashes."

So the czar reluctantly summoned one of his guards to fetch the whip. "Are you ready?" demanded the puzzled ruler.

"No, we must wait. I have a partner who should share the reward."

"A partner?" echoed the bewildered czar.

"Yes," the peasant answered. "When I came to your door, the general would not let me through until I vowed that he would get half my reward. So go ahead and start with him. Give him the first fifty lashes."

The czar ordered the general brought before him. "This honest peasant wouldn't dream of cheating you," the czar sternly said to the trembling officer. "He insists that you be given your share of his reward now."

So the general was seized by two guards and given fifty lashes.

Then the peasant spoke again:

"Father czar, the general is, after all, one of your loyal servants. I think he should be well paid. Therefore I won't accept any reward at all, and you can give him my share as well."

And so the general was given another fifty lashes.

But the clever peasant, who had amused the czar and also had taught an unforgettable lesson to the officers of the palace, was afterwards given a suitable gift of land and gold.

The Czar's Frog Daughter

A classic fairy tale in which the traditional Russian witch—the "Baba-Jaga-with-the-bony-legs,"—makes an appearance. The version is based on the retelling by Afanasyev, a Russian folklorist.

In a glistening castle in a far-away empire, there once lived a czar, his czarina, and their three young sons, who were as swift and as agile as falcons. The lads grew into handsome men, and when it was time for them to marry, the czar summoned them and said, "It is time for you to look for wives." The three sons nodded their heads in agreement.

"So, my children, take your silver bows, and each of you shoot one arrow into the air. And wherever your arrows land, there each will find his bride."

The oldest son aimed his arrow high, and high it went, disappearing into the clouds. Then it fell into the garden of the czar of another kingdom, just as that ruler's daughter strolled in the palace garden. She lifted the arrow from the grass, carried it to her father, and showed it to him.

"Give it to no one," ordered that czar, "except to the man who will take you as his wife."

Soon thereafter the oldest son rode by the garden. And when he spied the beautiful girl, he stopped and asked if she had seen a silver arrow.

"I have found what you seek," the lovely maiden replied. "But I will not return it unless you promise to marry me."

The prince proposed at once, and was of course accepted. Then he started for home, promising to return soon.

The arrow of the second brother flew lower than the clouds but higher than the forest that surrounded the castle. Falling in a neighboring prince's courtyard, it landed beside the princess of that kingdom.

She plucked the arrow from the ground and brought it to her father.

"It is a sign of luck," said the prince. "Give it to no one, except to the man who will take you as his wife."

Soon after the second son began his search for his silver arrow, he met the lovely princess. She showed him his arrow, and he at once asked her to become his wife. And promptly she consented. Then he started for home, promising to return soon.

The youngest son, whose name was Ivan Tsarevitch, now aimed his arrow into the air. It flew neither to the height of the clouds nor beyond the forest, but just far enough to glide above the houses that surrounded the castle. Then it fell into a swamp outside the village, almost striking a huge green frog that splashed about in the mud.

Ivan Tsarevitch came upon the green frog soon after he began his search. But the frog sat stubbornly on the silver arrow, refusing to budge. Ivan coaxed and begged and threatened, but the frog would not move. Instead it shook its head and croaked, "Ivan Tsarevitch, I will not return your arrow unless you promise to take me as your bride."

This puzzled poor Ivan. How could he possible marry a frog? Troubled and perplexed, he departed for home without his arrow.

When all three sons had returned, the czar questioned them: "Well, my lads, what brides have you found?"

The oldest son replied proudly, "I have found a czar's daughter."

"And I, a prince's daughter," the second answered.

Then it was Ivan's turn to speak. But he remained sad and

silent, unable to say a word. And when his father glared at him impatiently, he began to weep.

"Why do you sob, Ivan Tsarevitch?" the old czar asked.

"What can I do but cry?" Ivan replied. "My brothers have found such suitable brides, and I have found nothing better than a green frog. Tell me, father, must I take that ugly frog for my wife?"

The old czar stared at his youngest son and frowned until a hundred wrinkles formed on his forehead.

"There is nothing I can do," he sternly said at last. "That is your fate, and you must follow it. Go, my son, and marry the green frog."

And so it happened. All three sons were married—one to a czar's daughter, one to a princess, one to a frog.

Not long after the weddings, the czar was curious to see which of his daughters-in-law was the most talented. He summoned his sons and told them that their wives had only until the next morning to weave napkins for his banquet table. He would inspect their work on the morrow, and choose the best.

Ivan Tsarevitch returned home in tears.

"Why do you cry, dear husband?" croaked the frog.

"I cry because our father wants each of his daughters-in-law to weave a napkin by tomorrow morning. And how can you, a frog, do that?"

"Oh, don't weep and don't worry, dear husband," the frog replied. "Everything will be ready in time. Lie down and go to sleep."

As soon as Ivan fell asleep, the frog hopped twice, shed her green skin, and turned into a beautiful maiden. Into the courtyard she tiptoed, and whistled a strange tune. Maids and servants instantly appeared. They wove a dozen magnificent napkins, embroidering them with an eagle's crest. Ivan's wife then placed the twelve napkins next to her sleeping husband, slipped back into her skin, and was a frog once more.

When Ivan awakened the next morning he found the napkins alongside his bed. In all his life he had never seen more beautiful weaving or embroidery. Joyfully he delivered them to his father, who declared that these napkins were by far the most exquisite.

Then the czar issued a new command. "I want each of your wives to make a dish of buckwheat cakes," said he. "I shall taste them at breakfast tomorrow, and then decide which one of my daughters-in-law is the finest cook."

Ivan Tsarevitch again returned to his wife in tears. "Don't weep, dear husband," the frog said when she heard about the czar's second demand. "Lie down and go to sleep. I shall somehow manage."

But unbeknownst to Ivan Tsarevitch, his two sisters-in-law had followed him home. They peeked through the window, curious to see how a frog that had woven such magnificent napkins would cook a dish of buckwheat cakes. The frog, however, realized that she was being watched. *Ha!* thought she, *I will play a trick on my sisters-in-law!* She spooned some flour on a board, and leavened it; then she stirred it; then she heaped it; next, she jumped on the stove and lit a high fire. Directly into the fire she poured the dough. And, of course, it burned.

But the two sisters-in-law, who had watched the entire process with fascination, sped back to their kitchens and did the same, thinking that this was, perhaps, a splendid new way to make especially delicious buckwheat cakes. Naturally their cakes also burned, and were so foul to the taste that they could not be fed even to goats.

As soon as the frog saw her sisters-in-law depart, she hopped twice, slithered out of her green skin, tiptoed into the courtyard, and whistled her eerie tune. Immediately servants, cooks and kitchen maids appeared. She told them what was needed, and in moments they returned, bearing steaming platters of the sweetest buckwheat cakes imaginable. These she placed on a table next to her sleeping husband, and then once more donned her green skin and became a frog.

When Ivan Tsarevitch awoke, he saw the delicious cakes beside his bed. And you may be sure that the czar was particularly pleased when he tasted them, since the cakes his other two sons had carried to him had been so dreadful.

Now the czar announced that he planned a magnificent banquet for the next evening. "I want my sons and their wives to attend," he said.

Ivan Tsarevitch dreaded attending an elegant dinner party with a huge and ugly frog. So for the third day he made his way home with tears in his eyes. And again his wife told him not to be distressed. "We will somehow manage," she said. "You will go to the banquet alone. But when rain begins to fall, know that your wife is being washed in dew. And when lightning flashes, know that your wife is dressing in her finest clothes. And when thunder rumbles, your wife will appear."

Ivan did go to the banquet alone. His brothers and their wives were already there when he arrived, and as he took his seat at the table they began to jeer and joke and tease. "Why are you alone, Ivan

Tsarevitch?" they mocked. "Why didn't you bring your frog-wife?"

"Don't make fun of me," Ivan replied. "My wife will be here soon."

When the rain began to fall, Ivan Tsarevitch said, "Now my dear wife is being washed in dew." His brothers laughed, for they thought he was talking nonsense. But Ivan ignored them.

When lightning flashed a few moments later, he said, "Now my dear wife is arraying herself in her finest clothes." The two brothers shrugged their shoulders. "Ivan must be losing his mind," they snickered, winking at each other.

Then thunder suddenly rumbled with such force that the castle shook to its very foundations. Ivan walked to the window, peered out, and said triumphantly, "Here comes my dear wife now." A coach drawn by six prancing white horses drove up to the palace. From it stepped the most beautiful young woman anyone had ever seen. She entered the grand ballroom, walked to Ivan's side, and embraced him.

Soon thereafter dinner was served. The czar and the czarina, Ivan's two brothers and their wives, and even the servants could not stop gazing in wonder at the beautiful maiden. And they noticed an astonishing thing: she ate her dinner in a most peculiar way. She put one bite of food in her mouth, and the second one in her sleeve; then one spoonful in her mouth and the next in her other sleeve.

The wives of the two older brothers thought she must have a good reason for this, and decided to do the same. They also put one bite in their mouth and one in their sleeve, and then one spoonful in their mouth and the next in their other sleeve.

When supper was finished, all the guests went to the ballroom. While musicians played their harps and flutes, the czar asked his oldest daughter-in-law to dance with him. She refused, saying that the youngest of the wives should have that honor. And Ivan's wife danced so beautifully and lightly that it appeared as if her feet didn't touch the floor at all. Then she asked the czar if he would enjoy seeing some magic tricks. When he nodded his head, she shook her right sleeve, and the morsels of food that fell to the floor turned into a garden. In the garden stood a statue, and around it crept a cat. Slowly the cat climbed to the top of the statue, and there sang and told stories. Then Ivan's wife shook her other sleeve, and the morsels of food that fell from it turned into a bubbling stream on which six swans swam gracefully.

All the guests had gathered around and were watching in awe and fascination.

Then Ivan's wife waved her hand—and garden, cat, swans and stream disappeared instantly.

When the other two daughters-in-law danced, they too shook their sleeves. But to their horror nothing appeared but scraps of leftover food. Worse still, as they shook their sleeves, morsels of food flew all over the ballroom.

"Stop it, stop it," shouted the czar as he was hit on the nose by a chicken bone.

Turning crimson-red with embarrassment, the two wives apologized to the czar and his guests.

In the meantime, Ivan—who had never before seen his wife in human form—wondered how she had changed so miraculously from an ugly green frog into a magnificent maiden. While all the guests were dancing he hurried home, hoping there to find some clue to the mystery. Entering her room he found her frog skin on the floor. *If I can only get rid of that skin,* he thought, *my wife will never again become an ugly frog.* Quickly he tossed the skin into the fire and watched it burn in the flames. Then, pleased with himself, he returned to the ball and rejoined his wife.

But after the banquet, when they had returned home, Ivan noticed his wife nervously search high and low for the frog's skin. And when she couldn't find it, she asked:

"Ivan Tsarevitch, have you seen my coat?"

"Which one?"

"My frog's skin," she replied. "I threw it off here."

"And I burned it," he answered happily.

"Oh, Ivan, that is the worst thing you could have done," she wailed. "If only you had been patient for a few more days, I would have remained yours for all our lives. But now we must part, perhaps forever."

She wept bitter, bitter tears, and then she said, "Farewell, my dear. Search for me in the thirtieth realm of the czar, in the thirtieth foreign kingdom, where the evil witch known as Baba-Jaga-with-the-bony-legs dwells."

She clapped her hands once and was transformed into a cuckoo. Then the bird flew swiftly out an open window.

Ivan Tsarevitch grieved over his wife for many days, asking everyone he knew to tell him what to do. But no one could advise him. And so one day, Ivan took his silver bow, filled a knapsack with bread, threw a water flask over his shoulder, and went out into the world in search of the thirtieth realm of the czar, the terrible kingdom of the fearful, bony-legged Baba-Jaga.

Ivan wandered many, many days, and finally met an old man whose complexion was as white as milk. He asked the czar's son, "Where do you go, Ivan Tsarevitch?"

"I go where my eyes take me," replied Ivan, "to seek my wife. She is somewhere in the thirtieth kingdom where the Baba-Jaga-with-the-bony-legs dwells. I walk and I walk and I don't know where I go. Do you, old father, know? Do you perhaps know where the Baba-Jaga lives?"

"Certainly I know," the old man replied. "Why shouldn't I know?"

"Then tell me, good man, which direction I must take to get there."

"Why should I tell you, my son?" the old man answered. "It is all the same whether I tell you or not. You'll never accomplish what you have set out to do."

"Whether I accomplish it or not, old man, please tell me the way," Ivan begged. "Tell me and I shall be eternally grateful to you."

"Well, if it's that important to you, then take this ball," the old man instructed. "Roll it in front of you, and wherever it goes, follow it. It will take you right to the horrible Baba-Jaga-with-the-bony-legs. But when you get there, she's sure to eat you."

"Not me," answered Ivan. Then thanking the old man, he did as he was told. The ball rolled uphill and down, and Ivan followed close behind.

At last he came to a forest so dense the daylight scarcely penetrated. And there, right in the path the ball was taking, crouched a mighty bear. Ivan hurriedly put an arrow to his bow. But as he took careful aim, the bear rose on its hind legs and said, "Don't kill me, Ivan Tsarevitch. I will help you later on when you need me." Ivan lowered his bow, spared the bear, and then hastened after the rolling ball.

Deep in the forest Ivan next saw a plump falcon perched on the branch of a tree. Thinking that the bird would make a delicious meal, he again put an arrow to his bow. But before Ivan let the string snap and the arrow fly, the bird fluttered its strong wings and screeched, "Don't shoot me, Ivan Tsarevitch, I will help you later on, when you really need me." Hearing this Ivan lowered his bow a second time, sparing the falcon from death.

For many hours more the ball rolled and bounced through the forest, until it stopped at the very edge of an ocean, touching the tail of a fish stretched out on the shore. Now weak from hunger, Ivan seized the fish and was ready to cook it when it whispered, "Don't eat me, Ivan Tsarevitch, and I will help you later on when you need me."

So Ivan tossed the fish back into the ocean, and continued on his way.

At last he came to the thirtieth realm of the czar in the thirtieth foreign kingdom. There he noticed a little hut sitting on stilts; and if it had not been propped up by branches and boulders, it would most certainly have collapsed—that's how rickety the hut was.

Ivan entered. There on the stove sat the Baba-Jaga-with-the-bony-legs. Her feet rested on a bench, and her hideous head was hidden in the chimney.

"Welcome, Ivan Tsarevitch," she exclaimed. "Tell me, have you come here of your own free will or has someone forced you to undertake this journey?"

"By my will and also against my will," Ivan replied.

"Are you hiding from someone or are you looking for some-one?" the Baba-Jaga asked, waving her bony legs.

"I am not hiding, mother. Rather, I seek my dear wife, the green frog."

"Ah yes, ah yes," said the Baba-Jaga. "The green frog. She is indeed an ugly frog. You are silly to have come so far for her."

"Then you know where she is, mother," Ivan exclaimed. "You must tell me."

"She cleans my brother's house," the Baba-Jaga replied.

"And how do I get there?" Ivan asked.

"You must listen carefully, because I will tell you only once. I cannot repeat even a word of it. There is an island in the sea, and on it stands a palace. Enter the palace without fear, but as soon as you see your wife, grab her and flee. Do not look around you, above you or behind you, for if you do, misfortune and disaster will befall you."

"But how do I get there, mother? How do I get there?" Ivan asked.

"You will somehow find the way," the Baba-Jaga replied, and then would not speak another word.

Ivan thanked her and left. When he reached the ocean he peered out as far as he could, but nowhere could he see an island. His eyes filled with tears, and he grieved bitterly. Then the fish he had saved swam up to him and asked, "Why are you so unhappy, Ivan Tsarevitch?" Ivan told the fish that he was looking for an island in the sea. Without another word the fish beat the water three times with its tail. An enormous bridge rose from under the green waters—its supporting pillars made of silver, the railings of gold, and the platform of crystal. And the bridge led to an island.

When he reached the island, Ivan soon realized that he was separated from the castle by a forest as dense and thick as a wall. No matter how he pushed or pulled or pried, he could not force his way through. Weak from lack of food and rest, he sat down at the forest's edge, too famished and too exhausted to go on. Then he saw a rabbit leap by, pursued by the falcon Ivan had spared. The bird swooped down, killed the rabbit, picked it up in its beak and dropped it at Ivan's feet. After Ivan had broiled and eaten the rabbit, he felt his strength return. Once more he tried to penetrate the forest. But now the bear whose life he had spared lumbered towards him.

"Welcome, Ivan Tsarevitch," boomed the enormous animal, "what brings you here?"

"I must get to the palace," Ivan replied, "but the forest is too thick and I cannot get through."

"I will help you," said the bear, and he set to work uprooting trees. The great brown beast worked all that day and all that night without ceasing. And by the end of the second day, a narrow footpath all the way to the castle had been cleared.

"Now I must leave you," the bear said. "Remember—do not stay a minute longer than necessary."

Ivan gazed in astonishment at the castle. It was made entirely of glass, and when the sun shone on its high turrets they sparkled and reflected all the colors of the rainbow. Dazzled by the brilliance, Ivan shielded his eyes and slowly walked to the main gate. He tapped on the gate three times, and when no one answered he entered. The palace seemed deserted—except, that is, for a giant turtle nodding its head in greeting. Then Ivan realized that the turtle was beckoning him forward. The young man was slowly led down a winding corridor, past an iron door and past a silver door. When the turtle reached a room with a golden door, it stopped and nodded its head. Ivan opened the door, and in the room he found his lovely wife.

"My dearest one," she exclaimed, "you have arrived just in time. Tomorrow I would have been gone, and you would never have seen me again. Tomorrow I am supposed to marry the horrible brother of the Baba-Jaga."

Without waiting another moment they made their plans for escape. She again changed herself into a cuckoo, and taking Ivan under her wing flew away. And because they never looked back or around or above, but only straight ahead, they escaped from the dreaded and mysterious realm of the czar, from the thirtieth foreign kingdom and home of the Baba-Jaga-with-the-bony-legs.

When they reached their own kingdom, Ivan's wife became a maiden again. Then she explained that she was the daughter of a mighty czar, and that she had been transformed by the brother of the Baba-Jaga into a green frog because she had refused to marry him. The curse could be broken only by someone who would marry her as a frog, and tolerate her in that shape for at least thirty days. Failing that, she could be saved only were she rescued from the thirtieth realm of the Baba-Jaga. As Ivan Tsarevitch had done exactly this, she was now free and would forever remain in her human form.

And Ivan and his lovely wife lived happily for many, many years.

But the Baba-Jaga, who can be both a good and a bad witch, was not forgotten by the grateful couple. Because she had helped Ivan, he rode to the border of the thirtieth realm once a year. And each time he went he gave her a golden ball in remembrance of the enchanted ball that had led him to her hut.

What the Baba-Jaga does with the golden balls, nobody knows. However, strangely enough, children who live near her kingdom have told their parents that from time to time they see golden balls flying through the sky.

Could it be that the old Baba-Jaga is juggling them?

The Tale of the Pig

"Making fun of important people" is a favorite folklore subject. This classic tale from Caucasia laughs happily at a pompous general. The author is unknown.

n a little farm near a little village—far away, and just as long ago—there lived an old woman, her husband, and their friend. This friend, you should know, wasn't a man or a lady, a lad or a girl—the friend was a pig.

A most unusual pig! She knew how to grasp the handle of a bucket in her little mouth, walk all the way to the well, fill the pail with water, and return home. And that was not all—every morning she tidied the house; and at dusk each day she cleaned the pots and dishes, and then went to a stream to wash the soiled clothes and linens.

One day while the pig trotted toward the stream, carrying a neat little bundle of clothes to wash, she was spied by a prince who had been hunting in the forest. In quiet surprise he watched while the animal expertly soaked and scoured the laundry. Too astonished to say a word, he watched the pig cleverly hang the clothes in the sun to dry. And then the most amazing thing of all occurred—the pig stepped into the bubbling water and instantly changed into the most beautiful young woman the prince had ever seen. With tears in her eyes she recited,

"A girl I'll be
When a man weds me,
But this sad day
A pig I'll stay."

Then the maiden became a pig once more, gathered her laundry, and trotted home. The prince, who had not let her out of his sight for a moment, followed; and but a moment after the pig entered the little hut where she lived with the farmer and his wife, he appeared in the doorway. And he asked the old couple if they would give him a bed for the night.

"We are very poor," the old man replied, "and we cannot make you very comfortable. We can offer you nothing to eat or drink, and we have no extra bed."

"That doesn't matter at all," replied the prince. "Merely let me sit by the hearth all night." And there he stayed.

The next morning the prince offered the old man ten gold pieces for his pig. But the peasant shook his head. "I cannot, gracious sir," he said. "The little pig is all we have. We'd be lost if we gave her up." Then the prince offered the old man twenty gold pieces, and twenty gold pieces more each week for as long as he lived. Happily the peasant agreed. And the prince cradled the pig in his arms, and rode away.

As soon as he arrived at his castle he told his father that he wanted to marry the little pig.

"What has come over you?" the old king shouted. "How can you ask to marry a pig? You must be insane! Why else would you dare do such a thing? Do you want to disgrace our family? Everybody will laugh at us."

"Father, I must marry this pig," the prince replied. "You *must* permit it."

And so determined was the young prince that the king reluctantly consented to the wedding. But after the ceremony the king ordered his son and his bride to an old room in a hidden part of the castle, where neither the prince nor the little animal could be seen by anybody.

The prince was not at all distressed. Instead, once he was alone with the pig he gently said, "Now, dear wife, a girl you can be—for I have wed thee." And instantly the pig became the beautiful young woman the prince had seen at the stream. And so lovely and radiant was she that even the sun seemed to pale in her presence.

The prince then took his wife by the arm and led her to the king, who rejoiced when he saw the happy couple. And to show his complete approval, he placed a crown on the head of the girl.

But the tale does not end here! For although no one knew of this or saw him, the king's general had been peeking into the room when the pig became a beauteous maiden. And so impressed and envious was he that he thought to himself as follows·

"The prince found an ugly little pig, and magically he changed it into a young woman far more beautiful than any girl that any of us have ever seen. Well, why shouldn't I search out the largest pig in our country? And after I marry the pig, it will no doubt become the most beautiful girl on earth."

And so the general took leave from the court, and traveled the country over seeking a pig. And at long last he found one so enormous that it seemed more like a cow than a pig. But this pig was no bewitched young maiden—it was just an ordinary pig that knew nothing more than squealing, oinking, eating, and wallowing in the mud.

The poor general, however, bought it, and—pig in arms—mounted his horse. The pig squeaked and squealed, jumped down and dashed back to its sty. The king's general tried again. And only after a great struggle and much effort did he succeed in bringing the frightened animal back to court.

At the wedding ceremony the pig behaved frightfully. It rushed between the legs of the bridegroom and the guests, bumping and thumping them. But at last the ceremony ended. Then the general led the pig to his chambers and said, "Please, please turn into a young girl. You don't have to pretend any longer that you are something else. A girl you can be—for I have wed thee!"

But all the pig did was to bite the poor general's leg. Then off it rushed through the castle, into the fields, and finally to its happy life again with all the other pigs.

Thus ended the marriage between the general and the pig.

But every time the general saw the prince's lovely wife, he scratched his head in utter bewilderment, and hoped that the day might still come when his pig would return to him in the form of a beautiful young girl.

And with this hope, the king's general lived happily until the day he died.

The Peasant and the Waterman

Everyone receives his just rewards in this classic retelling by the great Russian writer, Tolstoi, of an ages-old fantasy.

n a clump of woods at the edge of a lake, a peasant chopped and chopped away at a tree—a fine old tree that would keep his fire going and glowing through all the long winter. Then suddenly the peasant's axe slipped out of his hands and fell with a splash into the water. Quickly he dove into the lake, hoping to find his precious axe, his only axe. But no matter how many times he swam to the bottom of the icy lake, no axe did he see.

"What can a peasant do without an axe?" he cried aloud. "How will I ever earn enough money to buy another?"

Then out from the lake came a *waterman,* one of those mysterious beings that live with the fish in rivers and lakes and streams.

"Tell me, good peasant," said the demon, "have you by any chance lost this axe?"

The peasant carefully examined the axe held by the *waterman.* Then sadly he shook his head. "No," said he, "this isn't mine." And indeed it wasn't, for the axe the *waterman* held in his hands was made of gleaming gold.

The *waterman* turned and dove underneath the blue surface of the lake without a word. But a moment later he returned, holding a sparkling silver axe. "Is this the one you lost?" he demanded.

"No," the peasant answered. "Mine was not so splendid as that."

Again the *waterman* descended. And this time when he reappeared he held the peasant's axe aloft. "Good peasant," he said, "I have

113

found your axe. And because you are so honest, I am going to give you all three."

The grateful peasant thanked the *waterman* again and again for his kindness, and then rushed home to share his good fortune with his wife.

But one of his neighbors heard his story, and decided that this was an easy way to become rich—for after all, thought he, an axe made of silver or gold is a great treasure. Off went the neighbor to the very same lake, and as soon as he reached it, he threw his iron axe into the icy waters. Then he sat down and loudly wailed.

Suddenly the *waterman* arose from the lake with a golden axe in his hand. "Is this perhaps your axe?" he asked.

Greedily the dishonest peasant reached out to grab it. "Yes," he shouted. "Yes! That's the one I lost."

The *waterman* did not say another word. Instead, he descended with the golden axe to the bottom of the lake.

The peasant waited. An hour passed . . . another hour. It grew dark. Night came . . . but the *waterman* never returned.

And so there was nothing left for the envious peasant to do but go home. Because he had been dishonest, he had lost even his good working axe.

Ivan and His Knapsack

Everyday familiarity with the Lord, St. Peter, Death and the Devil is a characteristic of the more primitive Eastern European folklore—as in this ancient Rumanian folk tale.

Ivan was a good and happy man who had served in the army since his youth. He had always been a good soldier, but as he grew older he was no longer able to keep up with the younger men. And so when he was sixty, he was given an honorable discharge from the service, and his captain presented him with two silver coins for traveling expenses.

Ivan marched off in good spirits—knapsack on his back, gun over his arm, two silver pennies jingling in his pocket—loudly singing old army songs.

It happened that the Lord and Saint Peter, who had come to pay a visit to earth, were walking the same road as Ivan. And they were disguised as beggars. When the Lord heard Ivan's cheerful voice, He smiled. "Here comes a good man, Peter. He owns only two pennies, but when he sees that we are beggars, he will give them both to us."

So it was. When Ivan passed, he gave each a penny, murmuring, "To give away what was given to one brings one closer to Heaven." And then he continued down the road, resuming his song.

Saint Peter was deeply impressed. "Old Ivan is truly a kind and generous man," he said, "and I should like to reward him."

"That can be done, Peter," the Lord replied.

They soon overtook Ivan, who was still marching and singing as merrily as ever.

"Good luck to you, Ivan," said the Lord.

"Thank you," Ivan replied. Then, spinning in surprise, he asked, "How do you know my name?"

"If I were not to know it, who would?" answered the Lord, smiling.

115

"No riddles, please!" snapped Ivan. "Who are you? Speak up!"

"I am first of all the beggar to whom you gave your last penny. And I am returning it to you now, for I have no need for money. I merely wanted to show Saint Peter that you have a kind heart. And to answer your question, Ivan—I am the Lord. And because I am pleased with you, I shall grant you one wish."

In awe, Ivan fell on his knees before the Lord. Then he said, "Dear Lord, if You will give me anything I want, then this is what I ask: please give me the power to order anybody I wish into my knapsack, not to come out until I so command."

The Lord did this for Ivan, and then said, "When the time comes, Ivan, that you are tired of roaming the earth, come to my heavenly gates and knock. They shall be opened to you."

"I will come with great happiness, my Lord," Ivan said, "but first I want to see more of the world."

With this Ivan left the Lord and Saint Peter, and continued with his journey. Near evening he saw an inn and asked the owner if he might stay overnight. The innkeeper saw that Ivan was a soldier, and could not pay, and so he led him to an empty room in the attic.

The room was not an ordinary one—at night it was inhabited by devils. Ivan, of course, did not know this. Tired from his long walk, he undressed immediately and went to bed. Just as he became comfortable, a demon pulled the pillow out from under his head and tossed it across the room. Ivan leaped out of bed, angrily grabbed his sword, and looked high and low for the mischief-maker. But the devil had made himself invisible.

Ivan was angry, but because he could find no one he returned to his bed and stretched out again. He had been asleep for only a few moments when he was awakened by frightening noises: the sound of a hundred cats meowing wildly in his room, then the growls of hungry bears, then barking dogs and grunting pigs. Now Ivan realized that he was in a room inhabited by devils. Quickly he seized his knapsack, opened it, and shouted, "Into the knapsack, devils, every one of you!"

Drawn by an irresistible power, one devil after another flew into the knapsack. When all were inside, Ivan tied a leather strap around his bundle of demons, shoved it under the bed, and was soon fast asleep.

When morning came and the devils had not returned to Hades, Satan's special assistant was sent to the inn to see what had happened. Seeing Ivan peacefully asleep, he walked over to the bed and slapped the old soldier. "What's this?" Ivan shouted. "Another one? Into my knapsack with you!" And the assistant devil found himself drawn into the bag, crowded in with the other demons.

Ivan went back to bed and slept undisturbed until ten o'clock. Then he arose, found a heavy cane, and began to give the bag and all the devils inside it such a trouncing that the innkeeper rushed upstairs to see what was making so much noise.

"Well," Ivan explained, "I fought all night long with the devils that lived in this room. Now I've got them all packed away in my knapsack and I'm giving them a thrashing they won't forget."

When he had beaten them for a while longer, Ivan opened the bag, and, one by one, took the devils out by their horns and gave each a sound beating. The special assistant devil was saved for last, and after Ivan had given him a particularly thorough whipping, the old soldier made the demons promise never to return to the inn. When Ivan finally loosed his hold on him, the special assistant devil tried to get away so fast that he lost his footing and fell on his face!

"God bless you, good soldier," the innkeeper said. "I can't tell you what it means to me to have my inn rid of those devils at last, and I want to reward you for your wonderful and heroic deed. I hope you will stay here as my guest for the rest of your life."

"Thank you for the offer," Ivan said to his host. "But I have other plans, and must leave now." He put his knapsack on his back, slung his gun over his shoulder, and marched away like the good soldier he had always been.

Ivan decided now that he would like to visit Heaven, but he didn't know how to get there. He took the silver penny the Lord had returned to him and kissed it, hoping that somehow this would bring him the answer. Instead, he found himself carried off so quickly that in but a moment he stood before the gates of Paradise.

"Who is there?" Saint Peter asked.

"It's me," Ivan answered.

" 'Me?' Who's 'me'?" Saint Peter asked, for though he really knew who it was, he thought Ivan was being somewhat impertinent.

"It's Ivan."

"And what is it you wish, Ivan?"

"I want to know about Heaven," Ivan said. "Do you have tobacco for my pipe?"

"No, Ivan, there is no tobacco here."

"Is there any wine?"

"There is no wine in Heaven," Saint Peter said, and he added, rather gruffly—because he was saddened by the things Ivan thought most important—"and you are asking too many questions."

"Just one question more. Where can I find all these things?"

"You can find them in Hell, Ivan. You will not find them here."

"Then I shall try Hell," Ivan said, "because Heaven doesn't have the things I like best."

And with this remark Ivan turned his back on Saint Peter and marched straight down to Hell. When he got to the gate he knocked and shouted.

"Hey, there! Do you have any tobacco?"

"As much as you want," someone replied from within.

"What about wine?"

"Certainly—there's plenty of wine."

"And gambling?"

"Of course! Why not?"

"Well," Ivan said, "that's all I wanted to know, and it sounds good. Come on now, hurry up, open the door."

The devil was delighted, and he opened the gate immediately. What a surprise to see old Ivan come marching in! When the devils saw him, still carrying his knapsack, they all moaned—for none of them had forgotten his meeting with Ivan at the inn, and all now trembled with fear. But Ivan just settled himself comfortably, and ordered the best tobacco for his pipe and some wine. What speedy service he received! The devils snapped to attention whenever he uttered a word, since none of them wanted to end up in that knapsack again!

The special attention he was given went to Ivan's head, and he became quite unruly. The demons were annoyed, but still so afraid of the knapsack that they scrambled to wait on him, hand and foot. Finally the situation became so bad that the routine order of things in Hell were completely upset, and the demons realized that they had to get Ivan out at all costs.

It was the devil's grandmother who offered the best idea for getting rid of their unwanted guest.

"Just get me a drum," she said, "and I wager that he'll soon be gone."

They got her a drum and on it she played the march that the army plays as it goes into battle. When Ivan heard this rat-tatta-tat tatta-tat he jumped to attention, grabbed his gun, and ran outside, for he thought a battle was beginning. And like any good soldier, he was ready to join in the fighting.

The moment he was through the gates, of course, the devils slammed and bolted them with their strongest locks and chains. And they paid no attention when Ivan knocked and howled for them to let him back in.

"I'll tear the gates down!" he shouted. But he couldn't, of course, though no one can say that he didn't try his best. Finally he realized that it was hopeless, and that he would never get back into Hell.

So Ivan decided to try Heaven again. When he neared the gates, he had an idea. "I don't really want to go in," he thought. "But I've been a soldier all my life, so why shouldn't I guard the gates of Heaven?" And he began this duty—though no one had asked him to—marching up and down in front of the gates of Paradise with his gun on his shoulder, proud of his new venture.

Soon Death arrived at the doors to get his new instructions from the Lord.

"Halt!" Ivan cried, and he pulled out his bayonet and pushed it toward Death. "Who are you, and where do you want to go?"

"I am Father Death, and I have come to speak to our dear Lord to find out what He wishes me to do."

"Not permitted to enter," Ivan said. "I will go myself, and bring back His orders."

"No, Ivan," Death replied. "I must go myself."

Ivan became angry when he saw that Death intended to disobey him. "No one passes here without my permission, including you, Father Death! Into the knapsack with you!"

Death had no choice, of course. But he moaned and groaned so loudly that Ivan began to worry, and at last he knocked on the gates of Heaven.

"Oh, it's you, is it, Ivan?" asked Saint Peter. "Have you traveled enough now? Are you ready to enter forever?"

"Not at all," Ivan replied. "I want to speak to our dear Lord. I have something important to tell Him."

"Enter, then, Ivan," Saint Peter said. "You are permitted to visit."

Ivan entered and marched directly to the Lord's throne.

"Lord," he said, "I have been serving you as a special guard at your Heavenly gates. Father Death arrived a short while ago, and he wants to know what your orders are."

"Tell him," replied the Lord, "that he is to return to earth. For the next three years, he is to put to sleep only very old people. Then he is to report back to me."

"Very good, my Lord," Ivan said. "I shall give him your message."

And Ivan turned sharply and marched back to his place outside the gates of Heaven. He opened his knapsack and let Death out.

"The Lord has commanded," he said in his most military manner, "that you return to earth, and for the next three years you will touch none but the very old. The young ones you must not lay a finger on, under any circumstances. Understand? All right, go and do your duty. Forward, march!"

Three years later Death returned, as ordered. When he saw the old soldier still standing guard, he said, "Tell me, Ivan. Do you intend to put me in your knapsack again?"

"I certainly do," Ivan said. "And not only that: I've thought about this a great deal since you were last here, and I've decided not to tell the Lord you've arrived. You are going to stay in my knapsack forever, because if it weren't for you no one would ever die. So into the knapsack, Father Death, and snap to it!"

A few days later the Lord paid Ivan a visit.

"Ivan," He said, "has Father Death not returned?"

Ivan hung his head in shame, afraid to look up, and made no reply.

"My Lord," Death said from the knapsack, "this guard has been making a fool of me, and has locked me up, as you can see."

The Lord opened the knapsack and set Death free. Then he turned to Ivan.

"Ivan," he said, "you lived your life as a good man. But since I gave you your special power, you have become proud and your ways have changed. Now I must stop you. The time has come for Father Death to claim you. And you must know, too, that his work is valuable. He exists for very good reasons, or I should not let him exist. You are very wrong to think the world would be a better place without him."

Ivan became very sad. He knelt humbly, and begged tearfully for three more days to prepare himself for death.

The Lord in His goodness granted Ivan's wish, and allowed him to return to earth for three days—without his knapsack.

When he returned to earth Ivan walked and thought about how he had spent his life. "Most of my life," he thought, "I was a soldier, and I liked that. But I never got anywhere. I was always poor. Then I went to Heaven, and to Hell, and back to Heaven. And I was a good guard when I returned to Paradise!" He began to become indignant. "It's not fair!" he thought. "All I am getting for my sacrifices and my long and faithful tour of duty is three more days of life!"

The more he thought about this, the sorrier he felt for himself. And finally, on the third day, he decided that he would play just one more trick. He took the two silver pennies that he had carried in his pockets all through the years, and used them to buy some wooden planks, a hammer, and some nails, so that he could make his own coffin. He had just put in the last nail when Death appeared.

"Are you ready, Ivan?" Death asked.

"Quite ready," Ivan answered, smiling.

"Then lie down in your casket, and be as quick as you can. There are many others waiting for me."

Ivan got into the coffin, but he lay down backwards, with his arms hanging over the sides.

"No, Ivan," Father Death said. "That's not the proper way."

"Like this, then?" Ivan asked, and he sat in the coffin sideways, with his legs dangling over one side.

"No, no!" Death said impatiently, for he was really in quite a hurry. "Get out and I'll show you."

So Ivan got out, and Death lay down in the casket. He closed his eyes and folded his arms across his chest. "This is the correct way," he said.

"Let me get a good look," Ivan said, and he pretended that he was carefully studying the way Death was lying. But instead he grabbed the lid of the casket, threw it on top, and quickly nailed it closed, with Death inside. And then he took it to a nearby river.

"Well," he said to himself as he watched the casket float slowly downstream, "now at last there will be no more death in the world."

Ivan did not know that Saint Peter had been watching him from Heaven. And Saint Peter went to the Lord and said, "Look, my Lord, at what Ivan has done to Father Death."

The Lord immediately had the coffin opened, and had Death come to him.

"Father Death," He said, "I am saddened by what Ivan has done. He must be punished, and I will ask you what you think is suitable. If I feel it is fair, you may carry it out, for all of Ivan's pranks have been at your expense."

What Death suggested was agreeable to the Lord, and Death returned to earth quickly and appeared before the startled Ivan, who had never expected to see him again.

"Ivan, Ivan," Death said severely, "you have only been able to make so much mischief because the patience and goodness of our Lord is unlimited. But now He knows that you need to be punished, and your punishment is in my hands. This is my sentence: I shall not fetch you for many, many years, and even then not until you have truly repented. It may be that you will have to live forever, even when you are so old and tired that you cannot talk or move, and wish only to join our dear Lord. And I can tell you that many days will come when you will fall to your knees and beg me to take your soul; and many times I shall say 'no.' " His speech finished, Death disappeared.

And so Ivan lived on for hundreds of years. Perhaps Ivan did truly repent, and Death was merciful to him. Otherwise, and for all anyone knows, the old soldier is still alive today.

Kristina and the Devil

How the devil is outwitted by a clever shepherd is the theme of this folk tale from Bohemia. Variations of the story have appeared throughout Europe for hundreds of years. The author is unknown.

In a small Bohemian village, in a tiny house with a pretty garden, there lived an old peasant woman and her daughter, Kristina. The girl was talented and beautiful, and you might expect her to have been surrounded by suitors. But the young men of the town stayed away from Kristina. She was known to have both a violent temper and a gift for saying nasty and insulting things.

On Sunday afternoons, as was the custom in the little village, the young men and their girl friends met at the inn on the village square to dance and sing.

But no one ever invited Kristina to dance, since her unpleasant, waspish ways were known to all in the village and even beyond. Thus she always stayed at home.

One lonely Sunday afternoon the girl decided to go to the dance by herself. What's more, she made up her mind to dance with *someone* that afternoon, even if it had to be with the devil himself.

She entered the inn, found a seat at a table, and watched and waited. It wasn't long before the door opened and a stranger in a green hunter's suit entered, smiled, and sat beside her. And shortly thereafter he began talking to her and invited her to dance.

When the villagers saw Kristina dancing with the newcomer, they laughed amongst themselves. "The poor man doesn't know what he's let himself in for," they whispered to each other, certain that in a moment or two the nasty-tongued girl would say something unkind to her friend, and lose him. But Kristina and the stranger danced merrily all afternoon without a cross or spiteful word. Never had the girl enjoyed herself so; and when the last dance ended, she said, "I wish we could continue dancing forever."

"Oh, but that can be arranged," replied the stranger. "Do you want to come with me?"

"Where do you live?"

"Put your arms around my neck," he replied with a smile, "and I'll whisper it in your ear."

As Kristina did that, the hunter instantly changed into a devil, and together they flew directly to Hades, the home of demon and devil.

When they reached the Black Gate, the devil rapped on it loudly. The door creaked open and in he went, carrying the girl on his back. Now the exhausted demon wanted Kristina to get off, but no matter how energetically he and his fellow devils pulled, or pushed, they failed to break her grip. Kristina clung to him with all her might; hadn't he promised that they would dance on and on?

Hearing her shrieks and screams, and the grunts and groans of the demons as they tugged and shoved, Lucifer himself rushed to the Gate to see what was happening.

The devil then explained that he had danced with the girl

in her village inn, and had tricked her into this journey to Hades. But never, he insisted, had he anticipated that the girl would cling to him and refuse to let go. In all his previous dealings with human beings, he said, it had been his experience that people wanted to get away from him as soon as they learned he was a demon.

As reasonable as this explanation may have sounded, it neither satisfied nor pleased Lucifer. "You are a foolish devil indeed," he said in icy tones. "You never remember what I tell you and teach you. You should know by this time that before you start dealing with human beings, you must understand their intentions. Leave here immediately—and don't come back until you have gotten rid of her."

Dismayed and humiliated, the devil now returned to earth

. . . still, of course, with Kristina clinging to him tightly, her arms around his neck. He promised her gold, money, a new house, diamonds, anything, if only she would let him go. But the girl just laughed. And for a devil, that is an insult indeed.

Thus it went for many hours. Then, on a road, the devil spied a young shepherd resting on a rock. Changing himself into human form again, the devil sat down beside the handsome young man.

"Whom do you carry on your back?" the shepherd inquired.

"Oh, my dear friend," the devil replied, "just imagine what happened to me! I was peacefully strolling down the road, minding my own affairs, when this woman suddenly appeared, threw her arms around my neck, and then jumped on my back. I've been trying to get rid of her ever since, but she won't let go. Now I'm on my way to the next village, where I trust I will find somebody who can pull her off. But I'm so tired that I fear I'll never get there. My legs have given out from under me, and I must rest."

Saying this, the devil moaned and groaned so sadly that the good-natured shepherd took pity.

"Listen, woman," the shepherd cried. "Let go of him and hang onto me instead."

When Kristina heard this, she promptly jumped onto the shepherd's back. Slowly he arose; quietly, carefully, without giving her a chance to see or feel his movements, he first slipped one arm out of the sleeve of his heavy fur-lined coat, and then the other. Next he opened the top button of the coat, then the second, and finally the third. And when the coat was loose, he suddenly twisted, twirled, and pushed. Kristina, who of course had not anticipated anything like this, went flying through the air, landing in a nearby pond.

The shepherd then returned to his flock of sheep, and found the devil awaiting him. "Good shepherd," the demon said, "you have done me an enormous favor. I might have been stuck with that woman 'til the end of time. I am going to repay you, come what may—even if I am the devil." And saying that, he disappeared.

Suddenly, a month later, the devil again appeared before the shepherd. "I am now going to show how grateful I am for the service you performed for me a month ago. Listen to me carefully. I am supposed to take a duke down to Hades on Tuesday night because he has treated his people so badly. That night you are to go to his castle. When you hear him shout and weep and rush about, you will know that the duke is fighting with me and pleading for another chance. At

that very instant you must come up to me and say, 'Leave immediately, devil! Otherwise it will go badly for you.' And I will obey you.

"The duke will be so grateful that he will offer you two sacks filled with gold. If he offers less, tell him that you will call me back.

"But this is not all. On Wednesday night I will be at the castle of another duke. There again you can come up to me and tell me to leave, and I shall. But on Thursday night, when the moon is full, I will appear at the castle of a third duke. There, good shepherd, you must not interfere, because *his* time is really up, and I must take him with me. And I must warn you, dear friend, that if you interfere on Thursday night, it will cost you your life."

And with these words, the devil disappeared.

On the following Tuesday night the shepherd went to the castle of the first duke. And when he heard shouts and screams he rushed inside, confronting the devil just as he was about to carry the duke through the door. "Leave here immediately," the shepherd said, "or things will go badly for you."

The devil instantly let go of the duke and disappeared. And the duke, who had indeed thought that his last hour had come, thanked the shepherd profusely and offered him two bags of gold.

The next night the very same scene occurred at a second castle, and again the shepherd was rewarded with two bags heavy with precious gold.

In the meantime the third duke, who had been threatened by the devil, heard about the young shepherd's exploits. Off rushed a messenger, begging the shepherd to come to the castle at once. But the shepherd remembered the devil's warning, and refused his assistance. Now the duke himself went to the shepherd, and swore that if his life were saved, he would ever after govern his people wisely and kindly.

"In that case," said the shepherd, "I will try to help you, even though it may mean that I will have to go in your place."

That night the moon rose full. The duke was dressed in a black cape and stood before the fireplace awaiting the arrival of both the devil and the shepherd. On the last stroke of twelve, the door mysteriously opened and the devil stood before him.

"Get ready," he said to the duke, "your hour has come." Without a word the duke followed the devil into the courtyard where hundreds of people had gathered to watch the eerie spectacle. Then the shepherd appeared and walked directly to the devil. "Leave quickly, leave quickly," he said, "otherwise things will go badly for you."

"How dare you stop me?" the devil demanded. "Don't you remember my warning?"

"Hush!" the shepherd whispered. "I care nothing about the duke. I am here to save you! Kristina is in that crowd of people. She will be here any second. If she grabs you this time, she will never let go!"

Zip! That's how fast the devil returned to Hades—forgetting the duke in his haste.

At first the duke couldn't believe his good fortune; but then he fervently promised his people that he would change his ways, and make life easier and happier for them.

And the shepherd?

He eventually married the duke's pretty daughter, and some years later became the ruler of the land.

And Kristina? Well, she had learned her lesson at last, and before long the beauty of her words matched the beauty of her face. Soon she married, and her life was filled with friendship.

How One Should Carve a Goose

The great writer Tolstoi always believed in the simplicity, cleverness and wit of the Russian peasant. Here is a humorous example.

Andreii, who was a poor but clever peasant, found one day that he had used up all his seed. And a peasant without seed is poor indeed, for then he will have nothing to grow and harvest, eat and sell. *I will go over to the landlord and see if he will give me some more,* said he to himself. And to enhance his chances of getting the precious seeds, Andreii roasted a fine goose, and carried it with him as a present for the landlord.

"I'll gladly give you some seed," the landlord said, "and to show you our appreciation for the excellent goose you have brought with you, we should like you to stay and have dinner with us. But tell me, how should I divide the goose, so that everybody in our large family gets a fair share?"

"I'll do it," Andreii quickly replied. He took a knife, cut off the goose's head, and gave it to the landlord, saying, "That is for you, because you are the head of the family."

Next he cut off the rump, and gave it to the landlord's wife. "This part, dear lady, is for you," he said, "because you always have to sit at home."

Then he gave each of the sons a leg. "And these are for you, because you are going to follow in the footsteps of your father." And the two daughters each received a wing. "I give you these," Andreii explained, "because when you get married, you will fly out of the house."

"Now all that's left is this little piece," said the clever peasant, pointing to the last part of the goose, "and I am sure that you won't mind if I keep it for myself." The good-humored landlord and his wife were highly amused by this sly behavior, and they laughed while Andreii devoured the plump breast and the other meaty, juicy parts of the goose. When he finished his delectable meal, the happy peasant loaded the seed onto his cart, and went home.

A few days later, however, the peasant's neighbor —who was rich and greedy, but not at all clever—heard how Andreii had obtained the seed without having to pay for it, and he decided to do the same. He immediately roasted five geese, and took them to his landlord. "Thank you for your present," said the landowner, "but with my wife and children, there are six people in this family. Do you have any idea how we can divide the geese so that each of us gets a fair share?"

The peasant thought hard and for a long time, but he could not find any satisfactory answer. And so the landowner sent for Andreii.

"Nothing is easier!" exclaimed the clever peasant when he was shown the problem. He took one goose and gave it to the landlord and his wife. "You, your wife and the goose makes three," he said. Then he gave one goose to the two sons. "And you two and this goose makes three." Next, he placed one goose before the two daughters, again saying, "The two of you plus one goose makes three."

This left Andreii with two geese. He took those, and joyfully concluded, "Isn't it wonderful how everything works out? For the two geese and I also add up to three."

When the landlord and his wife heard this, they laughed so hard that tears came to their eyes. Then the landowner rewarded Andreii for his cleverness with money and more seed. And the rich, envious peasant departed without any profit at all.

Radowid

Magic and mystery play an important role in the folklore of Slavic peoples, and this story from Slovakia is typical. It was retold by B. Němcova.

ong, long ago there lived a rich landowner who had never learned to save a penny. He liked to hunt and give parties, but alas—he did not like to work. So, as was bound to happen, he soon spent all his money. And because he no longer could afford to live stylishly in the city, there was nothing else for him to do but pack his bags and move with his wife and three daughters to a dismal, drafty old castle in the country. There they sorrowfully settled down to a life of poverty.

One day the hungry landowner went hunting and killed a rabbit. "This will make a splendid stew for us," he thought. But just as he was about to place the rabbit in his hunting bag, he saw before him an enormous bear. The growling beast rose on its hind legs, seizing the hunter with huge, furry paws.

"How dare you kill my rabbit?" roared the bear. "Because you did that, I am now going to kill you—unless you agree this very moment to give me your oldest daughter for my wife."

What was the poor man to do? He did not doubt that the bear meant its threat. So like the bargain or not, the landowner promised his oldest daughter away.

"In seven weeks I will come to get her," growled the beast, and lumbered off into the woods.

The landowner returned to his castle with a troubled heart, and when he saw his oldest child, he could not hold back his tears. His wife and the two other daughters hurried to his side, asking why he was so distressed. And after he related the strange events of the afternoon, they too began to wail and weep. Only the eldest daughter remained calm.

"Don't be sad, dear father," she said. "There was nothing else you could do."

Fearfully they waited out the seven weeks. And every waking moment of the day, the father searched for some way to save his daughter from her dreadful fate. Finally he decided to ask all his neighbors to arm themselves with clubs and daggers and bows, and hide in his home on the day the bear was to arrive. And then, if the bear did appear to claim his bride, they would pounce on him and kill him.

The people came, and waited. The sun began to set. And yet the bear did not arrive. Then, amid the stillness of the early evening, there could be heard the dim, far-off sound of music. And with each moment it grew louder and more enchanting. Suddenly the ground shook from the trampling of horses' hoofs—and out from the forest sped a long procession of golden carriages pulled by snorting stallions. They drove directly to the castle and halted in the courtyard. Six prancing chargers were harnessed to the finest carriage of all; and from it leaped a handsome young prince whose costume was woven from gold. Behind the prince there followed an entourage of soldiers, servants, lords, and ladies. The prince walked directly up to the landowner, bowed low, and in deep, courteous tones asked for his eldest daughter in marriage.

"I would like nothing more," replied the father. "But, alas, I have promised my daughter to a bear, and we are waiting for him right now."

"Bears should wed bears, and a beautiful girl like your daughter should marry a young man," answered the prince.

The landowner was easily persuaded, and his daughter was delighted. And so, behold! A dreaded wedding with a bear became a wondrous wedding with a prince.

The prince ordered that a chest of gold be taken from his carriage and given to his father-in-law as a present. And then the wedding was celebrated. Musicians played; the guests sang; acrobats performed; everyone laughed and marvelled at the turn of events, and all were prepared to dance until morning. But the prince insisted that he had to depart immediately. He bade a hasty farewell to all, and quickly climbed with his bride into the golden carriage. There was a fanfare from the trumpets, a flick of the whip from the driver of the carriage— and off they sped toward the woods, sparks flying from the galloping horses' hoofs.

After the procession had disappeared from view, the land-

owner and his neighbors waited fearfully for the arrival of the bear. But, happily, he did not come.

Now the landowner had plenty of money again, and his old habits returned. He gave fancy parties, bought foolish and elaborate finery, and wasted each day without ever giving any thought to the next. And as was inevitable, one day he again discovered that he didn't have a penny. Again he had to hunt for food if he and his family were to eat. So he took his bow and his arrows and went into the mountains. All day he searched without success; but then, as twilight descended, he spied a falcon circling high in the sky. The landowner took careful aim and his arrow sped to its mark; the falcon fell dead to the ground. Just as he was about to stuff the dead bird into his hunting bag, he heard a rushing wind—and an enormous eagle swooped from the clouds.

"How dare you kill one of my falcons?" the eagle screeched. "Because you are hungry, you feel free to devour one of us? Then I will eat *you,* cruel hunter! Unless, right now, you agree to give me your second daughter as my wife. Hurry, make your choice!"

And the unhappy landowner had to consent, because the savage eagle was already jabbing at him with his needle-sharp beak.

"I shall come for her in seven weeks," said the eagle, and off in a whirl of wind and flapping wings he flew.

134

The landowner was still in tears when he arrived home, bitterly reproaching himself for having bartered his daughter's life for his own. But she made every effort to comfort him.

"I will gladly marry the eagle, if that is to be my fate," she said.

Exactly seven weeks later, the landowner again summoned his neighbors to the castle. And again he plotted with them to kill the intruder when it arrived.

But the eagle did not come. Instead, just as the sun was about to set, there could be heard from the distance sweet music and laughter and the clatter of hoofs. Suddenly in the distance they glimpsed a procession of golden carriages flying toward them. Into the courtyard it came, and from the first carriage jumped a young prince dressed in the finest silks. He strode to the landowner, bowed low, and asked for the hand of his second daughter.

"There is nothing I would like more," replied the father. "But I have already promised my daughter to an eagle, and we are waiting for him now."

"An eagle should marry an eagle," the youth replied. "A beautiful girl like your daughter should marry someone more suitable."

The landowner consulted his daughter, and when she assured him that there was no one she would rather marry than this courteous, gentle young prince, her father consented.

Then the prince ordered that two chests of gold be given to his father-in-law as a present. And with many hurrahs, with dancing and song, the wedding was celebrated. But before an hour had passed, the prince announced that he had to leave. He said farewell to all, lifted his young bride in his arms, and carried her to his carriage. And as rapidly as they had arrived, that quickly did they go.

The guests, however, stayed, nor did they return to their homes until daybreak, for they feared that the eagle might still fly out of the skies to claim his bride. But he never appeared.

And now the landowner was rich once more, and again his old habits returned. And as had to happen, in only a matter of months his pockets were again empty, and he had to find food or go hungry. But this time he knew better than to hunt. He went fishing instead.

On his way to the mountain stream, he thought about his life, and grew ashamed of the way he had wasted his fortunes. Right then and there he decided that if ever he should become wealthy again, he would act more prudently. This time he would help people. He would give to the poor.

Lost in these thoughts, the landowner paid no attention to his surroundings, and only after he was in a thick forest did he realize that he had strayed off the path. But he continued on until he found himself in a valley enclosed by towering mountains. And before him was a calm, deep-green lake.

Thinking that he might just as well try his luck here, he cast his line. And very soon he had caught a good-sized fish. But before he finished unhooking it, the lake was awash with crashing waves—and an enormous fish thrust its head above the pounding, splashing surface. Its mouth was agape, and it was large enough to swallow not one but three men in a single gulp.

"How dare you kill one of my friends?" the fish demanded. "Now, cruel man, I shall swallow you. Unless you give me your youngest daughter as my wife."

This was a hard choice for the poor man, but when the gaping jaws of the hugh fish neared him, he saw no way out—and he promised away his youngest daughter.

"In seven weeks I will come for her." And with that the fish disappeared in the depths of the lake.

The youngest daughter did not seem at all upset when she heard the news. "After all," she said, "my sisters were not taken away by hideous animals, but by handsome princes. Perhaps I, too, will be lucky."

But this did not make her parents any happier. True—their other daughters had gone off with princes. But what had happened to them? Why hadn't there been any word from them since?

When the seven weeks were up and the fateful day dawned, neighbors from all around, young and old, came to the castle to protect the girl from the monstrous fish. Again they waited all morning and all afternoon, but the fish did not come. And then for a third time, just as the sun was about to set, they heard beautiful music from afar. As before, the ground shook under the stamping of horses' hoofs, and from the woods could be seen a stream of golden carriages speeding toward the courtyard.

The first carriage was again the most splendid. From it leaped a youthful prince who was even more lavishly clothed than the two other princes. Majestically he approached the landowner and asked for the hand of his youngest daughter.

136

"I would gladly let her become your wife, but I have already promised her to a horrible fish, and we are awaiting his arrival."

"A fish should have a fish for a wife," the prince replied. "Your daughter should marry a prince."

It didn't take long to persuade the landowner. And his youngest daughter was delighted to have so handsome a bridegroom.

With a motion of his hand the prince ordered three chests of gold brought from the carriages and given to his father-in-law. The wedding was celebrated there and then, and it was by far the most elaborate and the merriest of the three. But before an hour had passed, the young prince said farewell. He lifted his bride into the carriage and they drove off so rapidly that only a cloud of dust remained behind.

The neighbors stayed until dawn, ready to help the landowner defend himself against the fish if it came. But happily, the fish did not appear.

Now once again, the landowner was rich. But now he remembered the vow he had made against squandering his wealth. He lived thriftily and modestly with his wife in the old castle. But their days and nights were sad, made mournful by the memory of their three daughters. And the mother frequently wept because she was lonely, and because no word of their fate ever came.

Then the landowner and his wife were blessed with the birth of a son. The parents loved this child above all else, and they gave him the name *Radowid,* which means *welcome.*

The boy grew into a strong and handsome lad. But he never learned that his home had once been made cheerful and warm by three lovely sisters. Radowid's father had ordered that no one ever reveal the existence or the strange fate of the vanished girls.

One day, Radowid unexpectedly entered his mother's room, and found her weeping.

"Why do you cry?"

"That's the way it is, I am just sad today," she replied.

But Radowid couldn't understand. He went to his old nurse, who never refused him anything, and asked her the cause of these tears. At first she would not reply. But Radowid coaxed and insisted and wheedled and begged, and finally the good woman related the entire story. No sooner did Radowid hear it than he made up his mind to search for his sisters.

His parents implored him not to leave, for they were afraid that he too would never return. But Radowid had decided, and there was no stopping him. "I must find my sisters, even if they live in another world." And turning to his father, he asked for his finest horse and his mightiest sword.

When his parents realized that there was no way to dissuade him, they gave him money, a sword, a good horse and a servant. Thus armed, Radowid jumped on his horse, shouted farewell to his parents and his dear old nurse, and set forth into the world.

The young man and his servant rode into the woods from which the three princes had come. The road took them over mountains and through valleys to a dense forest, where the ground was so overgrown with twisting bushes and scraggy shrubs that each step became a struggle. Then all at once the horses halted, refusing to move even one pace forward. It was as if they were wooden horses nailed to the ground. They had reached an invisible line over which none but Radowid could step. Even his good servant, who tried to cross on foot, was held back by some magic power.

When Radowid realized that he was the only one permitted to cross the magic boundary, he turned to his servant and said, "It is clear that you are not supposed to go farther. Return home with my horse, give my parents my love and greetings, and assure them that I shall find my sisters."

The servant did as he was told. And Radowid went on alone. Slowly he made his way forward. He climbed two mountains in two days. But then when he thought that at last he was about to reach the top of a third peak, he found himself faced by an enormous, overhanging cliff. In it was a crack, and from the crack came wispy blue clouds of smoke.

A witch must dwell here, thought Radowid. *And somehow I must talk to her, because she may know what has become of my sisters.* He squeezed through the crack. Now, pushing and wedging his way carefully, he penetrated deeper and deeper; and the farther he pressed, the wider the opening became. Finally he was able to stand upright. Deep in the distance a spark glowed, and the nearer he approached it the brighter it grew. Finally he found himself next to a fire—and only then did he see the beautiful woman who played there with two small bears.

Gasping when she saw Radowid, she jumped to her feet. "I don't know who you are, or how you got here. Not even the birds ever enter. But you look like a good person—and so I must warn you. Go—go immediately. Don't stay another minute. For if my husband returns and finds you here, he will tear you to pieces."

"I have set out to find my sisters," Radowid answered, "and nothing frightens me. Don't ask me to leave. Instead, perhaps you can help me." And Radowid went on to tell the strange story of the disappearance of his three sisters.

Then the beautiful woman knew that this was her brother standing before her, for she was the oldest of the landowner's daughters. You can imagine the joy of her welcome and the questions each wanted to ask the other. But even as they embraced, a terrifying growl echoed through the cave.

"That is my husband," Radowid's sister whispered, and quickly she hid her brother under a tub in a corner of the cave.

"I smell human flesh," roared the bear, even from the distance. "'I smell human flesh!" he growled, rushing toward his wife, sniffing and searching and grunting ferociously.

"Dear husband, you are mistaken, no man has been here," his wife insisted. But the bear would not be convinced. He padded about the cave until he came to the tub under which Radowid was hidden. He overturned it. And there he found Radowid. He was just about to pounce on the young man when the clock struck the hour. At the stroke of seven the cave trembled and turned into a splendid castle. The bear lost his coat, and changed into a handsome prince. The two bear cubs became two fine boys.

And instead of tearing his brother-in-law to pieces, the prince embraced Radowid.

"You see," he explained, "a curse has been placed on me. I must live as a bear except for one hour a day, when I am allowed to be a man. The same curse has been put on my two brothers. One has become an eagle and the other a fish. It is our lot to war on humans wherever and whenever we find them. My people and my country have suffered the same fate. And it continues day after day, with no end in sight. We know only that we have been cursed because of our sister— but how we may be freed, and if ever, we do not know. If you should ever reach my brothers, ask them, for they may know more than I do. Now take these six bear hairs. If ever you should be in danger, just rub them and you will find six bears at your side to help you."

Radowid thanked his brother-in-law, and then asked the way to the bear-prince's brothers.

"My carriage is already waiting for you," said the prince. "The horses know the way. But you must hurry, for the hour of my bewitchment grows near, and as a bear I have no control over what I do."

Radowid said good-bye. Outside he found the carriage; as soon as he seated himself in it, it started flying like the wind over forest and field.

They reached the border of the bear's kingdom just as the hour of grace ended. Radowid was thrown from the carriage, and before his eyes the six magnificent horses shriveled into mice that scurried about and then ran into the forest. The carriage, in the meantime, turned into an empty nutshell.

Now Radowid was alone in a wild forest, but before him was a path to follow. After he had walked for many hours he found himself at an oak tree higher than any he had ever seen before. And as he looked up, he saw that just where it reached the clouds, a hut was perched on a twisted branch. He was quite sure that this was the home of his second sister. Quietly he waited to see if anyone would appear. But when it grew darker and nothing yet stirred, he called out and pounded on the trunk of the tree. A door opened in the hut, and from high above a beautiful woman shouted, "Who is making all that noise?"

"Your brother. Help me get up to you."

"Brother? I never had a brother," she answered. "But whoever you are, run away, for when my husband returns he will tear you to pieces."

"I am not afraid," Radowid replied. "Help me up, dear sister. I must speak to you."

And since she realized that the stranger had no intention of leaving, she threw him a rope. Quickly Radowid climbed it. When he reached the hut he saw that she cradled in her arms a fledgling eagle. Radowid explained as quickly as possible why and how he had come. Then the woman knew he really was her brother, and she embraced him tenderly. But while she was still expressing her joy, the tree began to tremble and sway, and the wind carried with it the swooshing sound of wings. The eagle was near.

"Quickly, brother, hide yourself in the moss," his sister directed.

And as Radowid did so, the eagle descended out of the clouds, screeching, "A man is here!"

"Oh, dearest, you are wrong. How could a man come here?" she asked sweetly.

"Well, if you won't bring him out, I will find him myself!" the eagle snapped, and he began to tear the moss apart with his powerful beak and claws. He had just come to the clump where Radowid crouched when the clock tolled the hour. At the stroke of seven, the hut in the tree turned into a castle, the little eagle into a playful youngster, and the eagle became a gentle prince.

This prince was also unable to tell Radowid what could be .done to break the horrible curse.

"You must find my youngest brother," he said. "Perhaps he will know what can be done. You will find my carriage below. It will take you to the farthest border of my country. There you will see a rocky road. Travel it as far as it goes, and it will lead you to a lake. Then wait until smoke rises from the water. When you see the smoke, dive into the lake.

"Finally, take these eagle feathers with you. If ever you are in danger, rub them. Six eagles will instantly appear at your side to help you. But now you must hurry, for my time as a human will soon be up."

Radowid's carriage traveled swiftly through the air; again, when they reached the border, the horses and carriage shrunk and shriveled before his eyes, becoming six sparrows and an eggshell.

Radowid found the rocky road the prince had described, and it led as promised to an emerald lake. At its shore he sat until two blue puffs of smoke rose from the water. Into the lake dove Radowid—but he neither floated nor sank. Instead, he found himself falling down a chimney, and with a resounding thud he landed on the hearth just as his youngest sister was throwing a log of wood into the fire. Frightened, she stepped back from the fireplace, and would have fled had not Radowid said, "Don't be afraid, I am your brother. I have come to help you." As they embraced the clock struck seven. The underwater house of reef, stone and pebbles gradually disappeared, a castle taking its place. Then her husband, the prince, entered in human form, because the hour from seven to eight was also his hour of grace.

"You have taken on a very, very difficult task," he told Radowid when he learned that the young man had come to save them all from their fate. "But perhaps you will succeed." And he began to relate the strange story of their enchantment.

"Many, many years ago an evil sorcerer visited our palace. When he saw our lovely sister he wanted to marry her. He pleaded and begged, but no matter how many wondrous things he promised her, she refused, because my sister could see into his evil heart. Then one day he warned that he would give her but one more chance to accept. And when she refused again, his rage was fearful. First he transformed us into beasts. And then he abducted our sister and took her to a hidden cavern in the ground, where she lies asleep on a silver bed."

Radowid listened intently. "But what must I do to free you?" he asked.

"You must enter his grotto," the prince replied. "Yet even to do that you must first find the golden key that hangs on a tree near its entrance. Should you succeed, you must then enter the cave and walk through seven strange and dangerous rooms. In the last of these the evil sorcerer guards the silver bed on which our sister lies. She is condemned to sleep without waking, and we are condemned to remain as beasts, until someone blows three blasts on the golden horn that hangs on the wall above the bed."

"I will do it," Radowid vowed. "I will succeed."

Then he kissed his youngest sister farewell, and the prince led him to the shore and showed him the direction he must take. Radowid walked until twilight gave way to dark night, and until black night gave way to gray dawn. Then before him loomed a tall oak tree, and from one of the branches near its crown dangled a golden key. Now Radowid knew that he had finally reached his destination. He began to climb. Up, up, up he went until he was within a hand's grasp of the key.

And then, just as he was about to seize it, the tree swayed and trembled. Clutching a branch, he looked down and saw six wild bulls charging at the oak and jabbing at its roots with their horns. Radowid remembered the hairs the bear had given him. He pulled them from his pocket and rubbed them together. Immediately six enormous bears appeared and tore the bulls to pieces.

Now Radowid looked for the ring once more. It had slipped to the end of a branch. Cautiously he edged his way forward. And just as he reached out to seize the slipping ring, a flock of wild geese appeared and violently pecked at his hands and face. Pulling the eagle's feathers from his pocket, he rubbed them together. Six eagles whirled in from the sky and drove the wild geese away. Now nothing stood in his way. Radowid grasped the key and clambered to earth.

He searched the ground for some sign of a cave, a door, or a keyhole. But none could he find. Under each blade of grass he peered, and not one pebble did he fail to raise—but there was nothing. Was this to be the end of his quest? Failure now, when he had come so far? In dismay and impatience he hurled the useless key at a moss-covered boulder. The instant the metal struck the stone, a door opened. Radowid entered the black cave; the rock door crashed shut behind him; but he inched forward. His first few steps brought him to a door made of ice. He wedged it open and entered the first room. It too was made of ice, and the air was so cold that for a moment he could not move. But he recognized immediately that he must not hesitate for an instant, for his feet were beginning to freeze to the ground. He gathered all his strength and with one great effort leaped into the second room. There mountainous flames awaited him, scorching his face and skin. He fled through in horror, only to find that in the third room hissing snakes covered the floor and walls. But Radowid leaped over them, and came to the fourth room, a lair of bats and screeching owls. And what he found in the fifth and sixth rooms we cannot tell you, for there are no names for the monsters that crawled toward him or slithered past him or plummeted from above. Yet through each of the rooms he passed.

And at last Radowid reached the seventh room. There the sorcerer sprawled on a throne, loudly snoring. Next to him was a silver bed, and on it the most beautiful girl Radowid had ever seen. And above the bed was the golden horn. As Radowid moved silently toward the horn, a clock struck twelve. The sorcerer stirred. Without opening his eyes, he asked:

"Are you ready to become my wife?"

143

And from the girl on the silver bed came a whispered but certain reply.

"No!"

"Then stay there and sleep for all eternity." And with that the sorcerer grimaced fiercely, and then returned to his slumbers and snores.

Stealthily Radowid crept to the silver bed and seized the horn. At the first blast the sorcerer leaped to his feet and flung himself at the young man. But Radowid dodged, and blew a second clear blast of the horn. And then a third, which seemed louder than a thousand claps of thunder.

With the last rolling echo, the sorcerer dissolved into a puddle of grease.

But now the lovely princess rose from her bed and with grateful tears thanked Radowid. And as their hands touched, they fell deeply in love.

Soon they were on their way to the castle of the youngest brother, where all his sisters and brothers-in-law waited for him. And then in a grand procession they hastened to the home of Radowid's parents.

Radowid married his beautiful princess that same day. But unlike the other wedding celebrations, which lasted for less than an hour each, this one continued for seven days and nights. So merry and joyous was it that from then on the word for "happiness" in Czechoslovakia became "Radost!" And to you, dear one, who need not fret about sorcerers or other nasty things, we also say "Radost!"

How the Carrot~Counter Got His Name

The most famous of all Bohemian and Silesian legends are about the mighty magician who punished wicked men, but helped children and people in need. These legends date from the Middle Ages, and were originally written down by J. Praetorius in 1662.

Far below the surface of the earth—far, far under the deepest wells or even the deepest of the seas—there once lived a mighty magician. His home was not, as you might suppose, a narrow cave or tiny hole. No, his lands stretched farther than your eyes can see, farther than an eagle can fly.

Palaces and fortresses could be found there; and in these majestic buildings were room after room crammed with treasures—heaps of rubies, diamonds, and sapphires, and vaults filled with gold and silver.

And the mighty magician's subjects were dwarfs, gnomes, elves, trolls, witches, and demons.

Although nearly all of his kingdom was underground, this magician did own a few acres of land in the mountainous region of Bohemia and Silesia. There he grew delicious fruits and vegetables and herbs.

Many years had passed since the magician had visited the upper world. But one fine May day, when the fields were covered with lovely flowers and the fruit trees were in bloom, he decided to come to earth again.

And the world was every bit as beautiful as he remembered it. The sun was brilliant, the air refreshing, and the colors of the trees and flowers dazzling. As he gazed about in admiration, the happy sounds of laughter and song reached the magician's ears. And at the

145

crest of a gentle hill he saw a group of girls weaving garlands of flowers. They placed these about each other, giggling and chattering and clapping their hands. Though all the girls were as charming and beautiful as spring itself, the magician's eyes soon fixed on one of them. She was Emma, the daughter of the Archduke of Silesia, and there was no question but that she was the loveliest of all.

So enchanted was the magician with her golden locks, her deep blue eyes, and her rose-red cheeks, that he immediately wanted to marry her. *But,* thought he, *she will most certainly reject me, since she knows nothing about me or about my lands beneath the earth.*

Poor magician! Had he only proposed to her right then and there, he would have saved himself much sorrow and bother. He would have learned that Princess Emma was already deeply in love with the Prince of Ratibor, and was soon to be married to him.

While the magician watched, Emma gracefully rose to her feet. "The sun is warm," said she. "I'm going to wade in the brook."

Now, thought the magician, *she will be on my property. That little stream belongs to me. And so I'll now be able to carry her down to my lands below the earth.*

No sooner had her toes touched the water than Emma lost her footing, and was pulled into the depths by invisible hands. All she could utter was a cry of despair. And by the time her friends rushed to the banks of the brook, Emma had disappeared.

When she awoke she found herself on a soft, silken couch in a bright and beautiful room. "Where am I?" she wondered. "Did I faint when I fell in that stream? Am I at the home of a friend? Or was I taken to a physician?"

She ran to the door, which opened easily. Then she hastened from room to room, perplexed by the silence and the absence of people. But as she made this tour she was awed by the magnificence and rich decor. Even Princess Emma had never before seen such splendor. At last she found great glass doors leading to a garden. Strangely-shaped plants spread their fragrance. Gaily-colored birds chirped charming songs and flew merrily from branch to branch of stately trees. The paths were covered with golden sand instead of pebbles.

Then as Emma walked through a rose arbor, a handsome young man approached. He bowed politely and smiled. "Welcome to my kingdom, gracious princess. I am happy to be able to offer you this palace and its parks as a gift. I shall do everything in my power to make things as pleasant as possible for you." These friendly words pleased Princess Emma, and her fear of her strange surroundings disappeared. She decided to accept the prince's graceful hospitality. Soon, she thought, he would explain how she had come to his realm, and soon he would take her home.

So Princess Emma lingered amid the marvels and splendor of the subterranean kingdom. Time did not seem to exist. For hours—or was it days or weeks?—she wandered through countless treasure chambers—and whenever she admired anything, the handsome prince would make her a present of it.

And she was well tended! A slight motion of her hand was enough to bring unseen servants to fulfill her every wish. At mealtime, delicacies were served on golden trays and set before her by invisible hands. Dresses spun of the finest silk, sparkling with gold and diamonds, filled her closets.

Yet it was not long before loneliness overcame her. And one afternoon, as Emma paced to and fro in the garden, sighing and sobbing, she confessed her sadness to the magician-prince. "I'd like to go back to my country, good prince," she said. "I yearn to see my friends and my . . ." But before she could finish, he interrupted. "Of course, of course! How foolish of me not to have realized that you are lonely. I will leave you for an instant, dear princess, and then return with a surprise."

He reappeared carrying a wand and a basket of carrots. "All

you need do is to touch a carrot with the magic wand and pronounce the name of your friend. And she will stand before you."

Emma immediately selected a carrot from the basket, touched it with the wand, and called the name "Vivian." And there before her was Vivian, her dearest friend. Joyfully they embraced. Then Emma called the names of other friends: Elizabeth, Mary, Cathy, Anne!

And soon all her favorites were with her, sharing the wonders and delights of the prince's kingdom. But then Vivian turned pale, and Elizabeth did not want to sing or dance. Cathy seemed to shrink and shrivel, and Anne turned yellow and could not move.

Frightened, Princess Emma raced into the gardens to find the prince, and back to her chambers she dragged him. She pushed open the door, and then the Princess Emma screamed. "My friends are gone. Now they are just ugly, withered carrots! How cruel! How shameful to play such a trick on me!" And Princess Emma fell to the floor and cried bitter tears.

The magician-prince gently stroked her silken hair. "I will gladly do anything for you, my dearest Emma. But some things are beyond even my powers. Your friends can live here with you only as long as the carrots live. I cannot make real people of them. But I can fetch fresh carrots for you, and then you can call all your friends back again." And off he sped.

But when he returned, his face was red with shame. "Forgive me," he begged, "but I cannot keep my promise. Although I've had my entire kingdom searched, my dwarfs could not find even one more carrot. However I have commanded that a great field be sown with carrot seeds. My servants are under orders to keep fires burning day and night beneath the fields so that the carrots will grow as quickly as possible. In three weeks they will certainly be ready, and then I will bring you as many as you wish."

"But I do not want to wait," the angry girl retorted. "And I do not wish to visit here longer. Take me home this minute."

"*Never!*" shouted the magician. And then he turned and pointed at a fortress in the distance.

"Watch!" he whispered. The fortress erupted into flames, collapsed on the ground in a heap of rubble, and then disappeared.

And then the magician turned to Emma. "Remember this well," he commanded. "You must *never* ask to leave!"

Emma nodded in silent fear. But at that moment she vowed somehow to make her escape.

148

A few days later the magician-prince announced that the carrots were growing nicely, and that very soon she would again be able to surround herself with her circle of friends. The frowning face of Princess Emma lit up at this news. And for the first time since she had arrived in the underground kingdom, the prince had the courage to express his long-desired wish. "Princess," he said, "make me happy and become my wife. My great kingdom and all my countless treasures shall be yours."

Since Emma was completely in his power, she was afraid to offend him in any way. Therefore she answered with beguiling friendliness, "Your offer of marriage is most unexpected, good prince. But I need time to think it over. First, however, you must prove to me that you really will fulfill all my wishes. Let us discuss this again after you bring me the carrots." The magician seemed more than satisfied with her answer, and departed in a merry mood.

Emma now thought day and night about her escape, and finally she devised a plan. First she caught a magpie in the garden, the very kind she had so often taught on earth to mimic a song or repeat a few silly words. And with great skill and patience, she finally succeeded

in teaching him to repeat this sentence: "The mountain magician has captured your Emma. Come in three days with your fastest steed to the mountain range. You can rescue her." And once this magic magpie had learned to speak, the princess trained it to fly up from the underground kingdom to the castle of the Prince of Ratibor.

Then Emma carried the magpie to the highest hill on these lands below the earth, kissed it on its tiny yellow beak, and sent it on its way. Up through caverns and cracks, through mines and chasms and caves it flew, until at last the magpie flew into the sun and sweet air of the earth. And then over fields and forests it winged until it finally reached the castle of the Prince of Ratibor.

At this very moment the Prince was deep in mournful memory of his vanished betrothed, and at first he paid no attention to the busy chatter of the bird on his window ledge. But then he realized that this was no ordinary bird. It was speaking to him, and it was speaking about his dearest Emma.

Now that he had heard the message, the prince ordered his best horse saddled, and he raced to Emma's parents to tell them the news and to plan his beloved's rescue.

Three days after the magpie had flown away, Emma dressed in her most beautiful clothes and jewels. A flame of joy glittered in the magician's eyes when he saw the lovely princess come toward him. "Beloved Emma," he said, "I have good news. The carrots are ready. And I hope, my dear, that you are ready to marry me, and that I will be rewarded for my efforts."

"Please be patient, dear prince," smiled Emma. "One more little wish of mine must still be granted."

"Merely tell me," he answered.

"My wedding," Emma continued, "should be. an occasion of great splendor. Feeling certain that this is also your wish, I want to be able to invite all my friends. Therefore I must know exactly how many carrots there are, and for each carrot I will invite one friend. Please, good prince, go into the field yourself and count them for me. That is the only way I can be sure there will be no error."

"Is this all you want, my dear one?" laughed the magician. "Indeed, it is a modest request for the prince of magicians. I am now the happiest carrot-counter on or under the earth." And with that he went to the fields.

"Count them carefully and exactly!" shouted Emma after him.

As soon as she was alone, the princess took a carrot she had secretly taken from the field herself, and changed it with a touch of her wand into a strong and fleet-footed horse. Then she swung herself into the saddle and gave the horse a light tap. The understanding beast galloped off like the wind, out of the imprisonment of the underworld and up toward freedom.

Meanwhile, the magician counted the carrots in the field. First he counted quickly so that he could quickly rejoin his princess. *But I must not be inexact,* he said to himself. *I am afraid that in my haste I made an error.* So he began to count the carrots again, row by

row. Arriving at a different total this time he knew he would have to count them once again. But alas, he ended up with yet a different number. And so he counted them over and over and over again until he reached the same number thrice. *One thousand, one hundred and one,* he said to himself. *Remember, one thousand, one hundred and one.* And repeating this and calling Emma, he hurried back toward her rooms in the palace.

"But why doesn't she come to meet me?" he asked himself. And he looked about for her. "Emma—where are you? *One thousand, one hundred and one. Emma—come here!*"

But nowhere was Emma to be found, and from nowhere did Emma come. And then fear and worry gripped him. "She has run away," he told himself. "She has most shamefully tricked me." And he shouted in anger and gnashed his teeth, and threw off his handsome princely shape, and emerged from the earth as a frightful giant.

From the highest peak of his mountain range he spied Emma fleeing into the distance with the Prince of Ratibor. In fury he hurled a rock bigger than a house at the fleeing pair. But so tired was he from stooping and bending to count the carrots again and again that the boulder fell short of its mark, and all it did was to raise a cloud of dust that shielded the princess and prince from the view and fury of the enraged magician. Safely they rode to their castle and were wed.

But back in the underworld the magician continued to storm and rage. Never did he want to be reminded of Emma again. Seizing vast boulders and masses of earth he covered the castle and its magnificent gardens from view. But on the surface of the earth, steep cliffs and deep crevices appeared, showing where far below the mighty magician was hurling boulders and prying rocks from their place. And the giant rock that was meant to block Emma's escape still lies in the mountains as a grim reminder of the terrible anger of the magician.

Bitterly disappointed in his love and in human beings, the magician now decided that he would have little more to do with the inhabitants of the earth. He left his kingdom even less frequently than before, and when he did come to earth it was always in disguise. Only when he heard of worthy men did he do good for them. Often he played tricks and pranks, and sometimes he severely but wisely punished the wicked. He decided that only children were worth having as friends. He became their protector, helper, teacher, and in some cases even acted as their father.

And on earth, the story of Emma's escape became so popular throughout Bohemia and Silesia that the people call this mighty magician who lives far, far below us "The Carrot-Counter." And that nickname has remained with him until this very day.

The Greedy Tailor

A dishonest artisan is taught a lesson he will always remember! This is still another legend about the Bohemian mountain magician, "The Carrot-Counter."

n one of the small towns high in the Bohemian Mountains there lived a tailor so skilled that customers came to him from far and wide.

His sewing was expert and the clothes he made were handsome and hardy. But—and this was a big "but" indeed—the tailor was dishonest. When asked how much silk or wool or satin he needed to make this coat or that suit, he always demanded more than was really required. Thus he was always able to keep a good piece of fine material for himself. Some of his customers sensed that he was cheating them, yet so delighted were they with the exceptional quality of his work that they did nothing to stop him.

One day an elegant young gentleman entered the tailor's shop, carrying a large package of fabric in his arms.

"I want you to make a hunting jacket with this red satin," he told the tailor. And immediately the tailor got busy. First he brought out drawings of the latest patterns, so that the gentleman could choose just the style jacket he wanted. Next he began his measurements. And finally, he measured the red satin brought by his customer. Then the tailor sadly shook his head. "My good sir, I have bad news," he said. "There just isn't enough material here to make the sort of coat you desire."

But the stranger—who was none other than the *carrot-counter* in disguise—yes, the mysterious magician who lives far below the surface of the earth!—was not fooled. He knew that not only had he brought enough material, but that in fact he had brought at least two yards extra. And so he snapped: "Of course there is enough material. And my coat had better be ready in two days, when one of my

153

servants will come to get it." And without waiting for a reply the elegant gentleman strode out the door.

Sure enough, two days later at the same hour a servant appeared in the store. And although the tailor had secretly stolen and stored away the two extra yards of fine satin, he whined and complained about the great difficulty he had had tailoring a coat with "so little material." Finally he boasted that only he, because of his great skill and experience, could ever have accomplished such a feat. The servant didn't say a word. He paid the bill, despite the fact that it was outrageously high, and departed.

A few days later the tailor had to visit a customer who lived in a lonely villa high in the mountains. The road was rocky, steep and untraveled. And the tailor walked as fast as he could, because he wanted very much to return to his warm, safe shop. But just as he turned a corner on the rocky path, he heard noises in the nearby brush. A huge black goat with immense horns loomed before him, and astride it was a fearful looking man. But what terrified the tailor most was the fact that the dreadful rider was dressed in the very red satin hunting jacket he himself had made just a few days earlier!

"So here we meet again," laughed the mysterious gentleman. "How fortunate—for this meeting saves me a trip to town. You and I still have to settle our accounts, tailor. Your bill was too high. And what's worse, you didn't deduct the value of the two yards you stole from me and hid in your closet. But now I am in a great hurry, so let us discuss this matter while I ride to my destination. Jump onto the goat— sit right behind me—and we'll talk."

How the cowardly tailor felt when he heard these words can well be imagined! He fell to his knees, raised his hands imploringly and whimpered, "Good and merciful master, I don't know how to ride. Please don't make me. I will gladly return the material to you, and I will also return all your servant paid me."

But the carrot-counter—for by now it was quite obvious to the tailor that the strange rider was none other than the mighty lord of the mountains—insisted that the tailor obey.

"Hurry! Mount the goat," he shouted. "If you don't do so immediately, my wrath will be even greater!"

Trembling, the tailor grabbed the tail of the huge, stamping goat, thinking that in this way he could climb onto its back more easily. But at that very moment the magic goat leaped from the ground and whirled high into the sky. The tailor shouted, screamed, and sobbed

with fear. And just when it seemed that he could hold on no longer, the goat descended rapidly, flew over a bog, and whipped the tailor loose. Plop! Down into the mud went the tailor. And when he finally crawled out, he was caked with mud, soaked with mud, spitting mud. And sneezing, coughing, dripping and oozing mud, he made his way home.

The next day when he started his work bright and early he was a different man. Never again did he steal material, nor did he overcharge. And soon he found that he was even more successful than before, because now a great many more people could afford to have their clothes made at his shop.

Through the lesson taught to him by the carrot-counter, the tailor became the most honest man in the entire community.

The Magic Walking Stick

Kindness is repaid a thousandfold by the magician who lives below the earth—"The Carrot-Counter."

From early morning until late at night, Alfred Ritter worked in a pharmacy preparing the drugs the doctors ordered.

But on his day off, whenever the weather permitted, the young apprentice wandered into the fields and valleys and collected rare herbs, unusual grasses, flowers and moss. On cold or wet days he stayed at home and read books about other lands, for it had always been Alfred's greatest desire to see the world. And by reading he at least learned about faraway places he would probably never be able to visit.

One beautiful autumn day Alfred walked to the mountains to collect some special herbs that bloomed at this time of the year. On his way home, he met an old, bent-over man with a snow-white beard who carried a heavy bundle of brushwood on his back.

"That wood is too heavy for you, good father," said Alfred. "Have you no son or grandson or friend or assistant to help you?"

"No, I'm completely alone," gasped the old man. "And if I don't want to freeze in the winter, I have to gather my firewood now."

"Then let me carry the wood for you," said Alfred, and he lifted the heavy load from the old man's back and put it on his own.

"No, I can't let you do that," wheezed the man through his bushy beard. "You see, I have no money, and I won't be able to pay you for your work."

"That's not what I had in mind at all," laughed Alfred Ritter. "I just want to give you a hand."

And so they trudged on together, neither saying a word. The old man seemed to know exactly where he was going, but for Alfred this part of the forest was new.

"What were you doing in the mountains?" asked the old man.

"Oh, just collecting herbs," Alfred replied. "I take great pleasure in collecting nature's beautiful things. But you know, good father, the one thing I would like to do more than anything else is to travel. I would go to the most beautiful places, I would climb the highest mountains, I would cross all the oceans. But, alas, this is just a daydream, because I can never expect to do even one of these things. After all, I am just a pharmacist's apprentice. And as you know, if one wants to travel, one needs time and money."

The old man listened attentively, but from time to time he seemed to laugh into his long white beard. Then he nodded. "That's youth, that's youth. Always restless, always anxious to see the world. But when you get as old as I am, you'll see that peace and quiet are the really important things."

At last they reached a splintered, tottering shack. The old man opened the creaking door and asked Alfred to enter and drop the wood next to the fireplace. Then he bent over the bundle and pulled a branch from it. "Here," he puffed, "take this for your trouble. It's all I can give you."

Alfred courteously thanked the old man and left. *It's kind of that poor old man to want to give me something,* he thought. *But what am I to do with this branch? If I throw it away, the old man may find it, and then his feelings will be hurt. Well, I'll simply carry it for a while, and use it for a cane.*

But after he had walked for a few minutes, Alfred realized that he was no longer following the path he had taken with the old man. He turned, planning to make his way back and ask for directions. But no shack could he find. And no old man.

Then Alfred knew he was hopelessly lost in the forest. *How am I going to find my way out?* he wondered. *The pharmacist must have a full day's work all ready for me, and now I am going to be late. Oh, how I wish I were home!*

And suddenly he found himself standing in the market square in front of the pharmacy, his cane in his hands!

What had happened?

Only a minute before he had been lost in a forest—and now he was home. *Perhaps this is a dream,* he thought. But in his hand he

158

held a stick, and with his other hand he could feel it. And there, leaning against the door and smoking his pipe was the pharmacist, nodding his head in friendly greeting. This was no dream!

Shaking his head in amazement, Alfred gazed at the mysterious cane. And as he did, he slowly realized what had taken place. The old man had been none other than the Carrot-Counter! And in return for the small favor given him, he had bestowed on Alfred Ritter something that would make Alfred's only wish come true. From now on Alfred would be able to travel the world, seeing the lands and the sights of his dreams.

To convince himself that all this had really happened, Alfred decided to test the cane's magic power. With trembling hands he clasped it and whispered, *Please take me to Venice.*

He was there. He was standing in the middle of St. Marco in Venice! People walked by, the pigeons clucked and pecked and fluttered, and the glowing white marble walls of the ducal palace were even more beautiful than he had ever imagined. In the distance he heard the calls of the gondoliers and the chimes of beautiful bells. Amidst all this splendor, Alfred stood, mouth open and rubbing his eyes in wonderment.

Then he remembered that he was expected at work. He again held the stick firmly in his hands and said, *Please take me back to my room.* And in the same moment he was back home, and nobody knew that he had been away!

This was the most wonderful secret in the world.

From that day on Alfred took advantage of every hour of free time. One day he would visit the top of the highest mountain in the world; on another day he would travel across the desert on a camel; on another he would hunt reindeer with the Eskimos.

He visited America. He learned the customs of the Chinese and Japanese peoples. He went into the deepest jungles of Africa and watched lions and giraffes grazing on the sun-drenched meadows and prairies.

And Alfred never had to worry about any danger because his magic cane would immediately transport him to safety.

And from every place and country Alfred visited, he always brought back one or two souvenirs.

Years passed and Alfred lived in his own world of adventure.

If anyone from the little town visited Alfred in his little room, the visitor was surprised to find so many wonderful foreign objects.

But when his friends asked him where he had obtained them, Alfred would never tell, but only smile. For he knew well that magic only lasts as long as it remains a secret.

Finally Alfred wrote a book about his adventures, and when the books became popular he earned enough from them to be able to give up his job. From that time on, his entire life consisted of travel.

When at last Alfred grew old, he decided to retire and return to his home town. And whenever friends came to visit him, they wondered about the old, worn and unimpressive cane Alfred held in his hands at all times.

"Why do you always carry that cane in your hands?" they would ask. But for many years Alfred never replied, only smiling when the question was asked.

One day, however, Alfred confided in his dearest and oldest friend. He told him the story of his meeting with the Carrot-Counter, and how in return for one simple kindness Alfred had been granted his greatest wish.

"Do you see, my friend?" Alfred asked. "All my happiness is due to this most unlikely looking cane. And now I am sure you understand why I have always guarded it so zealously, and have kept it near at all times."

After Alfred Ritter died, those of his friends who knew the wonderful secret rushed to his room to search for the magic cane. But nowhere was the cane to be found. It had disappeared forever, back down below the surface of the earth—far, far under the deepest wells or even the deepest of the seas—where the Carrot-Counter lives.

Plish and Plum

A story about children, puppies and the resulting mischief has rarely been more humorously told than in this 19th century classic German poem by Wilhelm Busch.

With a pipe between his lips,
    And two pups upon his hips,
    Jogs along old Casper Sly.
    How that man can smoke—oh my!
But although the bowl glows
Red and hot beneath his nose,
Casper's heart is icy-cold.
How can earth such mean men hold?
Casper says: "What use to me
Can such tiny puppies be?
Do they earn their keep? Oh, *no!*
Well, it's time I let them go.
Things not useful, fling away!
Have no sentiment, I say!"

At the water Casper stands,
"Now I'll drown these pups," he plans.
Frightened puppies squirm and shake,
For they fear the deep, green lake.

Splash! Into the pond one goes,
Tail end first, and then his nose.
Swoosh! The second follows suit,
Takes the same unpleasant route.

"That's well ended," Casper squawks,
Steals away and homeward walks.

But it happens—and here too!—
Things don't end as they seem to.
Paul and Peter—so 'twas fated—
Naked in the bushes waited
For a swim. And they could see
Casper's heartless villainy.
Like two frogs they dive, kechunk,
Where the poor young dogs had sunk.

Quickly each one with his hand
Drags a little dog to land.
"Plish, I'll call my dog," said Paul.
"Plum," said Peter, "mine I'll call."

Paul and Peter, spirits high,
Pet and stroke each puppy dry,
Then with speed and joy past telling,
The brothers streak home toward their dwelling.

Daddy Fittig, calm and cozy,
Mama Fittig, round and rosy,
Arm in arm sit peaceful there,
Troubled by no fret or care.

As their suppertime is near,
They know their sons will soon be here.
When the boys come into view,
Plish and Plum are with them too.
But Papa thinks all dogs a pest,
"No," he cries, shouts "No," with zest,
But Mama then with soft looks pleaded,
"Let them, Fittig!"—and succeeded.

Now comes dinner, so delicious!
On the table stand the dishes.
Hungrily they rush indoors,
Plish and Plum ahead of course.

Gracious! Look! Right in the cream,
Go eight wee paws! A two-dog team!
And the noise their lapping makes,
Shows what comfort each pup takes.

Through the pane peeps Casper Sly,
Chuckles loud and says, "My! My!
This is very bad—hee-hee!
Very bad, but not for me."

The Story of Flying Robert

What child will not decide, when told to stay in-doors, that it would be more fun outside? This poem first appeared in Germany in 1845, written by Dr. Heinrich Hoffman.

When the rain comes tumbling down,
In the country or in town,
All good girls and all smart boys,
Stay at home and play with toys.
Robert thought, *No, when it pours,*
It is better out of doors.
Rain it did, and in a minute
Bob was in it.

Oh, what wind, and how it whistles
Through the trees and through the thistles!
His red umbrella it has caught,
A nasty lesson he is taught,
For up he flies, right to the skies,
And no one hears his screams and cries.
Cold winds whirl him through the air
Cold rains soak his curly hair.

Soon they get to such a height,
They are nearly out of sight,
And his hat flies up so high,
It hits a cloud that passes by.

No one ever lived to tell
Where Bob stopped or where Bob fell.
Only this one thing is plain,
Bob was never seen again.

The Story of Johnny Head-in-Air

"Watch your step" is a familiar warning called by parents all over the world to wandering children. Here is another tale in verse by Dr. Heinrich Hoffman.

s he trudged along to school,
It was always Johnny's rule
To be looking at the sky,
And the clouds that floated by.
But things that just before him lay,
In his way,
Johnny never thought about.
So that everyone cried out,
"Look at little Johnny there,
Little Johnny Head-in-Air!"

Running just in Johnny's way,
Came a little dog one day.
Johnny's eyes were still astray,
Somewhere in the sky, away.
And he never heard them shout,
"Johnny, there's a dog, look out!"
And with one tremendous bump,
Down they fell with such a thump,
Dog and Johnny in a lump.

Once, with head high in a dream,
Johnny walked beside a stream,
Johnny watched the swallows trying

166

To see the cleverest at flying.
Oh my! he thought, what lovely fun
It is to watch the bright round sun,
Going in and coming out,
And that was all he thought about.
So on he strode, and in a wink,
He reached the river's very brink,
Where the bank was high and steep,
And the water very deep;
And three fishes in a row,
Stared to see him coming so.

One more step! Oh sad to tell!
In poor Johnny headlong fell.
And the fishes in dismay,
Flapped their tails and swam away.
There was Johnny on his face,
Floating near his writing-case;
Two strong men heard Johnny's cry,
Just as they were passing by,
And with their sticks these two strong men,
Fished dripping Johnny out again.

Oh, you should have seen him shiver,
·When they pulled him from the river.
He was in a sorry plight,
Soaking wet, he was a fright.
Wet all over, everywhere,
Clothes and arms and face and hair;
Johnny never will forget,
What it means to be so wet.

And the fishes one, two, three
Are coming back again to see.
Up they came the moment after,
To enjoy the fun and laughter,
Each poked out his little head,
And to tease poor Johnny said:
"Silly little Johnny, look—
You have lost your writing book!"

Max and Moritz

Every country in the world has its mischievous and lovable youngsters. Max and Moritz are the German ancestors of "Dennis the Menace." The poem is by the great satirist Wilhelm Busch in Germany in 1865.

It's Easter time! It's here again!
And the baker, with his men,
Has cooked all sorts of lovely things—
Buns and gingersnaps and rings.

When the baker leaves his store,
He wisely shuts and bolts the door.
Max and Moritz stand outside,
They want the cake that's locked inside
There's only one thing they can do—
They wriggle down the chimney flue!

They're in the store—now look at them:
They're sooty black from top to stem!
They crawl around the dim-lit shop
'Til in a flour bin they flop.
Now see them sneezing, chalky white—
Poor Max and Moritz—what a sight!
Then high upon a shelf they spy
A sugar treat they want to try.
They climb up on a chair to see
If they can reach it, cautiously.
Then crack! The chair splits! Down they go
And splash! They're in a vat of dough!

They stand there, covered with the dough,
They wonder what to do—oh, no!
The baker comes! He's heard the noise!
He'll teach a lesson to those boys!
"In here you go!" they hear him shout.
A pile of dough he flattens out,
He covers Max and Max's twin
HE BAKES
A CAKE
WITH BOYS WITHIN!

The boys don't whimper, they don't whine,
They think the baker's trick is fine.
Inside that cake they gnaw and chew
Till out they come! They've eaten through!

Despite himself the baker chuckles,
Raps them lightly with his knuckles,
Laughs and says, "No one but you
Could be a cake and eat it, too!"

Max and Moritz and the Tailor

*Wilhelm Busch illustrated his accounts in verse
of the pranks of Max and Moritz—who probably
served as the models for Hans and Fritz, the
Katzenjammer Kids.*

hrough the town and country round,
Mister Goats was most renowned.
Weekday clothes or evening gown,
Frocks, tuxedos, coats for town,
Gaiters, breeches, hunting suits,
Waistcoats and great leather boots,
A list of things too long to mention
All claimed Mr. Goats' attention.

If ever a fabric needed patching,
Darning, sewing, pressing, matching,
Piecing, hemming, or a fold
To make something new of something old,

Anything of any kind,
Anywhere, before, behind,
Mister Goats would do the same,
For that was Mr. Goats' great aim.
Therefore all the population
Held him high in estimation,
So Max and Moritz did invent
Some horrid tricks to plague the gent.

Right in front of the tailor's dwelling
Ran a stream, bubbling, swelling.
A road led to the stream's steep banks,
One crossed the bridge on wooden planks.
Max and Moritz, naught could awe them,
Took a saw when no one saw them,
Ritze-ratze, fiddle-diddle,
They sawed the planks across the middle.

When their job was finished well,
Suddenly was heard this yell:

"Come out, old Goat, old bearded billy,
Old goat, you are a four-hoofed silly!"
Now Goats could stand all sorts of jeering,
Jibes and jokes in silence hearing,
But Max and Moritz with their verse
Infuriated him, or worse,
And wild with anger, up he started,
With his yard-stick out he darted,
For once more that frightful jeer,
"Bearded billy!" rang loud, rang clear.

With one great leap, the bridge Goats makes,
Then *crash!* Beneath his weight it breaks.
Into the water plops the tailor,
"Hoorah," shouts Max. "Goats is a sailor!"

While Max and Moritz go skeedaddling,
Along the stream two geese come paddling.
Goats splashes, thrashes, also sneezes,
Then by their tails these geese he seizes.
And with one goose in either hand,
He flutters out upon dry land.

But afterwards he did not find,
Things exactly to his mind.
Plain it was that Goats had caught,
A dreadful sniffle, all for naught.

Oh noble Mrs. Goats! she rises
Fully equal to the crisis.
With an iron steaming hot,
She makes Goats warm where he was not.

Soon 'twas heard throughout the town,
"Good Mister Goats, can't keep him down."

The Fox and the Clever Wren

In this story from 18th century Germany, the greedy fox is taught a lesson he will long remember. The author is unknown.

 fox who had eaten nothing for two long weeks came to a tree where a wren had her nest. Desperately hungry, he shouted, "Wren, give me one of your young ones at once—or I'll knock down the tree with my tail and gobble up all of you."

The wren was frightened by this threat, but before she replied she thought the situation over carefully. Then she answered, "My dear fox, you might just as well leave my children alone. They are still so thin and tiny they would never satisfy your hunger. If you really want to eat a pleasant meal, just follow me. I will see to it that you get as much food as you can eat."

"All right," said the fox. "But no tricks. And if you don't keep your promise I'll come back and have all of you for my dinner."

The wren left her nest and flew slowly down the road, the fox trotting behind. After the bird had flown a mile she saw two women resting in the grass. And beside them were two baskets filled with delicious pastries.

Fluttering weakly, the bird circled slowly above the women and then seemed to fall to the ground, where she acted as if she were hurt and unable to fly. When the two women saw the wren they wanted to catch it and care for it and take it home to their children. But the bird somehow stayed a hop and a flutter away from them—neither so close that they could capture it, nor so distant that they gave up the chase. While the two women were dashing after the wren, the fox crept to their baskets and stuffed himself with pastries. Then as soon as the

176

wren saw him chew the last morsel of his splendid meal, she rose high into the air and sped back to her nest.

About an hour later the fox returned to the tree where the wren lived. "My dinner was fine," said he, "but I'm not finished with you yet. Now, you must get me something to drink."

"Simple enough," chirped the wren. "Just follow me."

And again the bird flew down the road, trailed by the fox. Soon she spied a man driving a wagon-load of wine barrels. She landed on one of the kegs and began to peck away at it. "Shoo," the driver shouted. "Go away." But she continued to peck. "Shoo!" he screamed. "Or I'll hit you with my axe." The wren continued to ignore him, peck-peck-pecking even harder. Furious, he swung at her with his axe. She ducked the blow; the axe struck the barrel, chopping a hole in its side; and out gushed wine. The fox ran behind the wagon, his mouth open wide, and drank to his heart's content.

"Are you satisfied?" asked the wren.

"Not yet, not yet. Now I must see something funny so that I can laugh."

"All right, follow me," whistled the clever wren.

She flew directly to the rafters of a barn where two farmers were at work. The wren perched on a beam high above the floor, and alongside her the fox balanced himself, and together they watched the two men, one old and the other young, busy at their tasks.

Suddenly the wren hopped off the beam, circled, and then landed on the old man's bald head. "Ouch," he cried, and grabbed for the bird. But away she winged. The farmer muttered and sputtered; then, just as he was ready to start working again, the wren descended once more to her perch on his bald and shining head. This infuriated the farmer, and he called to his companion, "Quick, hit the bird!" His co-worker struck at the wren with his thrashing flail. She hopped away. And instead of hitting the bird, the flail struck the poor old man full on the head.

High up in the rafters the fox laughed so heartily that he lost his footing and fell to the floor. The two angry farmers lost no time in giving him a sound beating. Only with difficulty did the fox manage to escape from them at all.

The wren, satisfied with her work, flew back to her nest.

At last there will be peace, she thought. *I doubt very much that Mister Fox will want me to get him anything else.*

And the wren was right. The fox never appeared again.

A Gift for a Gift

"Honesty is the best policy" is one of the most popular and lasting of all folk tale themes. The original version of this story is attributed to Saxony, and it dates from the 17th century. The author is unknown.

mighty king once lost his way while hunting alone in a forest, and late at night, when he was cold and weary and hungry, he at last reached the hut of a poor miner. The miner was away digging for coal, and his wife didn't realize that the gentleman who rapped on her door and begged for a night's lodging was the king himself.

"We are very poor," she explained, "but if you will be content, as we are, with a plate of potatoes for dinner and a blanket on the floor for a bed, you will be most welcome." The king's stomach was empty; his bones ached; and he knew that on this dark night he would never find his way back to his castle. And so he gratefully accepted the woman's hospitality. He sat down to dinner with her and greedily ate a generous portion of steaming potatoes baked in an open fire. "These are better than the best beef I've ever eaten," he exclaimed. And still smacking his lips, he stretched out on the floor and quickly fell fast asleep.

Early the next morning the king washed in a nearby brook, and then returned to the hut to thank the miner's wife for her kindness. And for her trouble he gave her a gold piece. Then he was on his way to his palace.

When the miner returned home later that day his wife told him about the courteous, kind and distinguished guest who had stayed overnight in their home. Then she showed her husband the gold piece he had given her. The husband realized at once that the king himself must have been their overnight guest. And because he believed that the king had been far too generous in his payment for their humble fare and lodging, he decided to go at once to present his majesty with a bushel of potatoes—fine, round potatoes, the very kind the king had enjoyed so much.

The palace guards refused at first to let the miner enter. But when he explained that he wanted nothing from the king—that in fact, he had come only to give the king a bushel of potatoes—they let him pass.

"Kind sire," he said when he finally stood before the king, "last night you paid my wife a gold piece for a hard bed and a plate of potatoes. Even if you are a great and wealthy ruler, you paid much too much for the little offered you. Therefore, I have brought you a bushel of potatoes, which you said you enjoyed as much as the finest beef. Please accept them. And should you ever pass by our house again, we will be happy to have the opportunity to serve you more."

These proud and honest words pleased the king, and to show his appreciation he ordered that the miner be given a fine house and a three-acre farm. Overjoyed by his good luck the honest miner returned home to share the news with his wife.

Now it so happened that the miner had a brother—a wealthy brother who was shrewd, greedy, and jealous of anyone else's good fortune. When he learned of his brother's luck, he decided that he too would present the king with a gift. Not long before, the king had wanted to buy one of the brother's horses. But because he had been asked to pay an outrageously high price, the king had never bought the animal. Now, thought the avaricious brother, he would go to his sovereign and

179

make him a gift of the horse. *After all,* he reasoned, *if the king gave a three-acre farm and a house to my brother in return for a mere bushel of potatoes, I will probably get a mansion and ten acres for my gift.*

He brushed the horse and polished its harness, and then rode to the palace. Past the sentries he walked, directly into the king's audience chamber.

"Gracious sir," he began, "not long ago you wanted to buy my horse, but I placed a very high price on it. You may have wondered why I did so, great king. Let me explain. I did not want to sell the horse to you. I wanted to *give* it to you, your majesty. And I ask you now to accept it as a gift. If you look out your window you will see the horse in your courtyard. He is, as you know, a magnificent animal, and I am sure that not even you have such a fine stallion in your royal stables."

The king realized at once that this was not an honest gift. He smiled and said, "Thank you, my friend. I accept your kind gift with gratitude. And you shall not go home empty-handed. Do you see that bushel of potatoes there in the corner? Well, those potatoes cost me a three-acre farm and a house. Take them as your reward. I am sure that not even you have a bushel of potatoes in your storeroom with so high a value on them."

What could the greedy brother do? He dared not argue with the king. He simply raised the heavy sack to his shoulders and carried it home, while the king ordered the horse put in his stables.

The Iron Box

*The shrewd peasant who outwits both his wife
and the authorities is the subject of this 18th
century folk tale from Württemberg. It is told with
inimitable Swabian gusto. The author is unknown.*

arly one cold morning—even before the sun had risen—a
poor peasant trudged into the forest to cut wood for his
stove. To his surprise he came upon an ancient woman, her
skin as wrinkled and crinkled as a walnut, and her hair as
white as an onion slice. And she crouched atop an iron box.

"Dear man," she whined, "I have been under an evil spell for
more than three hundred years. This box is hard and my old bones
ache, and I long to be free. If you will only march about me three times,
barking like a dog, the spell will end. Then you may take this box home
with you. It is filled to the top with coins. But there is one condition. Do
not tell anyone about the iron box. If you do, it will be your misfortune."

The peasant thanked the old woman, circled her thrice, barking and yipping as he marched. Off she jumped and hobbled away.
And onto his cart he loaded the iron box, and went home.

"Wife," he shouted when he reached his house, "I have something here that I am forbidden to discuss. But since you are my wife, I
am sure that this condition does not apply to you."

"You are right, husband," the woman replied. "A man must
tell his wife everything. And you may rest assured that my lips will be
sealed."

"Well," he chortled, "our money troubles are over. I found an
iron box filled with coins. But you must keep quiet about it."

They dragged the box down into their cellar and opened it.
Yes, just as the old crone had promised, it was filled with coins of silver
and gold. The peasant seized a handful and gave them to his wife. "Buy
meat for our dinner," he said. "We haven't tasted meat for two months."

181

Soon the mouth-watering aromas of a sumptuous repast wafted toward the home of their nearest neighbor. That woman could not contain her curiosity, and rushed to her friend to find out what was going on.

"Good day, neighbor," said she. "What are you cooking that smells so delicious?"

"Ah, my dear," the woman replied, "I am not supposed to speak of it, but I know that you are no gossip. When my husband went to the forest this morning to cut wood, he found a large box filled with money. And so we have fine meat for dinner tonight."

"Why, that's wonderful," the neighbor replied. "You may rest assured that I will tell no one of this."

But only an hour later the peasant's sister-in-law came by. "Sister," she shouted, "I've heard that you've had some wonderful luck. Tell me about it. You can be sure that your secret will go no farther."

And before the sun had set on that very same day, the news of the money box had traveled as far as the magistrate. This official called the peasant before him, and said, "Your wife has revealed that you have a chest filled with gold coins in your cellar. You must have stolen it. Bring it here."

"No, honored sir," the peasant answered. "I have stolen nothing. I am as poor as a churchmouse, but I am an honest fellow. And as for my wife, I thought you knew that she was slightly out of her head."

But the magistrate wasn't taken in by this story. "The court meets in two weeks. We'll see then how crazy she is."

What was the peasant to do? Who would believe his story? *Woe, oh woe,* he moaned to himself. *Misfortune has indeed befallen me. We peasants should keep our wits about us at all times.* With that, he returned to his home, stealthily filled his pockets with coins, hitched his horse to a cart, and drove to another town. Stopping at the largest bakery, he bought all the buns in the shop. Then he again went home and peeked through a window. His wife was busily cooking in the kitchen. Now he strewed the grounds around his house with buns. He even threw several buns on the roof, and tossed a few in front of the gate. Then he dashed into his home, screaming with anger. "Wife, you are just like all the other women. No sooner do we have a little money than you are too lazy to do any work. The Good Lord has rained buns on our home, and you do not even bother to bend down and pick them up."

"You must be out of your mind," replied the woman. "Whoever heard of it raining buns?"

"Go and look for yourself, lazy woman!"

The woman peered out of the window. And when she saw thousands of buns strewn all over the yard, she rushed out and spent the next three hours picking them up.

The next day the peasant said: "Listen, wife, when I was in

the city yesterday, I learned that our king has a new troop of soldiers with noses as sharp and long as bayonets. When they go for a march they practice stabbing people, and apparently they especially like to stab women. I understand that today they will be coming our way To save you from harm I will place our large iron washbasin over you— then they will not find you. And I myself will hide in the cellar."

"Hurry, hurry," cried the frightened woman. "Hide me, dear husband." And so the peasant covered her with the washbasin. Then he went into the chicken coop and let all the hens run into the yard. Next he scattered grain around and on top of the washbasin—and—*peck, peck, peck* against the metal went the bills of the chickens as they consumed the grain.

About an hour later the peasant raised the washbasin, and told his wife that the soldiers had left.

"Oh, it was terrible," sobbed the trembling woman. "I almost died of fright when I heard the soldiers' iron noses go *peck, peck, peck* against the basin."

"Well, it's all over now, and we are safe," replied the peasant. And with that the matter was ended.

Two weeks later, when the court was in session, both husband and wife were present. The peasant denied ever having found an iron box. But when his wife was questioned on the same point, she solemnly swore that all had happened just as she had described it to her neighbor.

"Do not believe this poor woman, sir," the husband interrupted. "She's slightly out of her mind. When was it, wife, that I brought the money chest home?"

"Don't you remember?" she answered. "It was the day before the Good Lord rained buns in our yard . . ."

The peasant looked at the magistrate with a slight smile on his face, as if to say "Just as I told you." And the magistrate looked back with an expression of sorrow, as if to say, "I sympathize with you, good peasant."

"Am I not right?" the peasant asked the magistrate aloud. "Isn't it unhappily obvious that my dear wife is crazy?"

"Crazy?" screamed the woman. "Don't you remember, husband, that you found the box just two days before our king's new soldiers with their long, sharp, iron noses marched through the village

184

and came to our yard? Don't you remember the terrible noise, the *peck, peck, peck* they made with their bayonet noses on the washbasin under which I was hiding?"

The peasant again turned to the magistrate, and shrugged his shoulders helplessly. "You are right," said the magistrate. "Your wife has lost her wits. Take her home and make sure that she causes no harm."

And so the peasant was freed of all his troubles. And the peasant's wife? Well, she changed, you may be sure. Never again did she talk out of turn.

The Golden Chain

The real value of a person lies in what he is—not in his outer appearance. This fairy tale, told in many versions throughout Europe, comes from Germany. The author is unknown.

ong, long ago, if you had happened to walk down a certain street in a certain little town, you might have passed a busy blacksmith's shop. In it worked the smith himself, pounding on his great anvil. And there alongside him were two of his three sons, each strong and swift in his duties.

But if you saw the blacksmith's third son, his youngest, you might have laughed aloud—for John was more likely to hammer his thumb than a nail, and more apt to trip than to walk quickly from the bin to the forge.

The plain fact was that John was always lost in daydreams— very strange dreams of demons and lost kingdoms and heroic deeds.

185

Try as he might, he could not put these thoughts out of his mind for a moment. But his impatient brothers and his busy father could not understand this; they called him *Dumb John,* and soon they would not permit him to work in the shop. Only the unpleasant tasks were given to the youngest son.

As the years went by, and the blacksmith grew older, his arms began to ache and his shoulders pained. And so one day his eldest son said, "Father, give me the forge. I am old enough and experienced enough to be the blacksmith." And the father replied, "Yes, the time has come for one of my sons to be the new smith. But how am I to choose between the two of you who work with me? You are both strong and both capable. I love you both and I cannot show any preference.

"So," the father continued, "both of you must go into the world. Exactly one month from today, when the sun rises golden in the east, you must return. And whoever brings back a chain that exactly fits around the forge—a chain that is neither too long nor too short—shall inherit the forge. In this way I shall test how keen are your eyes and how strong is your determination. Now look at the forge very carefully, because you are not allowed to measure it."

Far in the back of the shop, where he was sweeping up the day's litter, John heard this conversation. "Father," he asked, "may I not also go into the world and try my luck?"

John's two brothers laughed aloud. "Poor dumb John," they scoffed, "why waste your time? You are much too stupid and clumsy to ever find such a chain. And even if you did, you would certainly trip over it and fall in a river and drown! Stay home and keep the floors clean instead."

But the old blacksmith smiled at his youngest son and said, "I'm afraid that what your brothers say is true, my boy. Nevertheless, you may also go into the world. Perhaps you will even learn something away from home."

So all three brothers readied themselves for their trip. They said good-bye to their father and to each other. One brother walked toward the east, the second toward the west; and poor John, waving farewell, stumbled and fell, and then headed north.

After many days he came to a great forest. Because his feet ached and his legs were tired he stretched out under a tree and fell asleep. When he awakened—he didn't even know how long he had slept—a green-skinned woman stood beside him. "Where are you going?" she asked. "And from where do you come?"

"I seek a chain," he said, "that will fit my father's forge. But I am afraid that I shall never find one, since everyone tells me that I'm not at all clever. That's why they call me 'Dumb John'."

"Don't worry about the chain, dear John," the green-skinned lady replied. "I will help you find one if you come with me."

John followed her until they came to a part of the forest so thick with bushes and twined with twisting vines that they could go no farther. But there at the foot of an enormous tree was a cave. The green-skinned lady quickly stepped down into the cave. "Follow me," she whispered. Once inside she lit two candles. "Wait here," she said, and then deeper into the cave she went, soon reappearing with food and drink, and with straw for a bed for John.

"Eat well," she said. "Sleep long and soundly. When all your strength has returned, I will ask you to help me."

John slept for many hours. And when he awakened, he felt strong and confident. "I am sure," he said, "that today I will find a chain to fit my father's forge."

"Not today," said the green-skinned woman. "Today you must begin a task for me. It is something that only you in the entire world can accomplish. You see, dear John," she continued, "I am an enchanted princess. This ugly black cave was once the finest palace on earth. And you alone can free me and my kingdom from the evil spell with which we have been cursed. Have you not often dreamed of this? Didn't you sense that someday those strange thoughts would come true?"

"Yes!" John whispered. "What must I do?"

"For three nights you must stay by yourself in this cave," answered the green-skinned princess. "Between the hour of midnight and one o'clock, ghosts and spirits will whirl into the cave. They will tempt you and torment you, but you must not say a word to them, no matter what they do or threaten. If you should speak—even if it be only a single word—then you too will become enchanted, and both of us will be lost for hundreds of years. Are you willing?"

"Of course," replied John. "At home I learned how to endure hardships and remain silent. It won't be much worse here."

And so he stretched out on his bed of straw and slept quietly until a clock far in the distance struck twelve. Instantly the cave resounded with a terrible howling and clamor. Strange spirits—their bodies like those of men, but with heads of lions, tigers and monkeys—flew over to John and dragged him to his feet. In roaring voices they

asked him why he was in the cave. When he made no reply they threatened to throw him outside, where hungry wolves howled. But when he didn't protest they laughed, insisting that they had only been joking— that they were friends who would teach him how to change words into rubies, sounds into silver, songs into gold. But John didn't utter a word. Now he let himself be pushed and shoved and knocked and kicked. Then, just when it seemed that he must shout in pain, the clock tolled once. The spirits and ghosts disappeared as mysteriously as they had come. John crept back to his bed and in aching exhaustion fell asleep. Gone were the monstrous bats, the wild figures cavorting about with heads in arm, the huge and ugly frogs, the strange birds and reptiles—gone completely, and John was not interrupted in his sleep, although in his dreams the weird creatures still trumpeted and bellowed.

The next morning the princess arrived at the cave with four servants. He noticed that her skin was no longer quite as green as it had been the day before. Deftly and quietly she and her hand-maidens cared for his bruises and revived his strength with food and medicine. Then when the evening star rose she said, "Tonight it will be worse. But if you do not weaken, you will become a mighty king." And with these words she departed.

Once again he slept until midnight noises awakened him. Then, to his astonishment, he saw dozens of young men before him who looked exactly like him—were dressed in clothes like his—seemed to *be* him. And looming above them was a vast owl, who croaked, "Which of you is the real John? Speak up, and I will tell you all the secrets of the universe."

"I'm the real John," the real John almost shouted—but then stopped. Furiously the spirits pulled his hair, tripped him, pushed him and punched him and pinched him and pummeled him. But John kept his lips clamped tight—and when the clock struck one, all became quiet.

John awoke the next morning to find the princess standing beside his bed with six maids. He noticed to his amazement that her skin was now almost white. Only a few blotches of green were left on her arms and legs and on one side of her face.

"Just one more night," she said, "and then everything will be over. I will be free—free to be your queen. But now," she continued, "you must rest." And all that day the princess stayed at his side, salving his wounds and restoring him with food and powerful potions.

And indeed, this last night was the worst, for the spirits

changed the appearance of the cave from stark black stone to the familiar blacksmith shop at home. Three of the spirits took the shape of John's father and brothers—and all pretended they would help John if only he would speak. And how he wanted to cry to his father and his brothers for help, for the other spirits turned into huge bugs that snapped at him, biting and stinging, buzzing and screaming.

Desperately he closed his eyes and held his fingers to his ears. Weak and tormented, he fell. Barely opening his eyes he saw that he was now in a magnificent golden bed, in the most beautiful room he had ever seen. Bright sunlight streamed through the open windows, and as he looked out he saw a peaceful park aglow with flowers. *Another trick,* he thought. *I must be strong!*

Then a beautiful young woman entered the room, followed by twelve maids. She was dressed in billowing pink, and on her head she wore a sparkling tiara made of gold and precious stones. She walked to John's side and kissed his forehead. Then she placed a glorious golden crown on his head.

"What music does the king wish played?" she asked.

I must not speak, he said to himself. *If I do, all is lost!*

Then the princess laughed. "John," she said, "you may speak at last. Truly you may. I am the princess you saved, and now you are the king and master of my kingdom. It exists again, John—with all its people—thanks to you!"

But still he would not utter a sound. Then a clock tolled— twice, three times, four, seven—eight! It *was* true—he *had* saved the princess. With a shout of joy he arose; the princess threw her arms around him, and kissed him tenderly. Then as trumpets blared triumphantly the two young people descended a long staircase that led to a vast hall, and there they were married.

A few days passed. And then, suddenly, John remembered the chain he was supposed to bring back to his father. Tomorrow the month would be up! And tomorrow his father and brothers would laugh and sneer at "Dumb John."

"My dear husband, why are you so sad?" the queen asked when she noticed his distress.

"Tomorrow the month is up. Tomorrow my brothers and I are to return home. And I have no chain to bring back. I am still foolish, clumsy, stupid John."

With a quiet smile she left the room and returned moments later, a golden chain in her hand.

John was overjoyed. He decided to leave for home at once. His wife was ready to accompany him, but he wouldn't permit it.

Quickly he changed into his old drab and dusty clothes. Into his pocket he stuffed the chain. And then he set out for home.

When John arrived, his two older brothers were already there. Each had brought back an iron chain, but neither fitted the forge. One was too large, the other too small.

Now John walked toward the forge. *Here is where I always used to trip,* he said to himself—and he tripped, while his brothers roared with laughter. He steadied himself, and then walked on. *Here is where I often caught my sleeve*—and *scrricchh!* poor John ripped his shirt again. Now even his father joined in the scornful laughter. But then John took the golden chain from his pocket. It fit perfectly. When his two brothers saw this they were so envious and angry that they seized John and locked him in the chicken coop. Having thus taken care of their brother, the two young men continued their rowdy merry-making.

The queen, in the meantime, had followed John right to his house. When she heard the wild laughter she entered, walked up to John's old father, and asked what was taking place. He told her that his three sons had returned from a lengthy trip and that all of them had brought back chains for his forge. But curiously enough, he said, the chains of the two older and more clever brothers did not fit the forge, while the chain brought by his youngest son—"the stupid one"—circled the forge perfectly.

The queen then asked the old man if she might meet the youngest son. Embarrassed by this request the old man had to admit to the shameful behavior of the two older brothers.

The queen then immediately went to the chicken coop and opened the door. From it, along with hundreds of fluttering chickens, emerged poor John.

"Is this how a king is treated?" she cried angrily.

Hastily John washed and changed into the regal clothes his wife had brought him. Then they returned to the blacksmith's house.

The two brothers were still celebrating when the royal couple entered. Everyone in the room bowed his head in deference. No one recognized John, so different did he look in his regal attire.

The queen then said to the two brothers, "Look closely at your king. He is your brother—the very person you locked in the chicken coop."

When the two brothers realized that the king was indeed their brother, they began to tremble. Then they fell on their knees and asked for mercy.

And John, who was gentle and generous, pardoned them, admonishing them to be kinder in the future.

Then he and the queen bestowed many wonderful gifts on the old blacksmith.

The next morning, the royal couple returned to their palace, where John ruled his people justly and wisely for many, many years. And his two brothers, having learned their lesson, worked in the shop.

I'm glad to tell you that they became the best blacksmiths in the land. One called himself "Dumb Hans" and the other called himself "Dumb Willie"—and only you and I—and John—have ever known why.

It's Already Paid

The "practical joker" and his dupes make a comedy team anywhere in the world. What happens when the "gullible man" is not quite as gullible as he looks, however, is the theme of this humorous 19th century Austrian folk tale.

t sometimes happens that a farmer will work long and hard, and that nevertheless all will go wrong. The wheat does not grow, the apples are small and bitter, the vegetables twisted and stunted. Having harvested this kind of poor crop, a farmer who owned both a cow and a goat decided to sell his cow. The money he received would pay for new seeds for the next crop.

As he wearily trudged along the road, leading his cow to the city market, he was seen by three students who loved to play tricks.

Two of the students quietly stole down the road toward the market. But the third walked up to the farmer. "Tell me, good farmer," he said politely and seriously, "where are you taking that goat?"

"My *goat?*" asked the farmer, stunned by the student's ignorance. "You must be foolish indeed if you can't tell a cow from a goat."

"I know the difference between the two animals," the student smugly replied. "And what you—"

But the farmer wouldn't let him finish the sentence. "You obviously *don't* know the difference," he interrupted. "My goat is at home. This is a cow."

"No," the student answered calmly, "you must have taken the wrong animal. I know a goat when I see one, and that's a goat."

Saying this, the young man turned and walked away without giving the farmer another chance to respond.

At the next turn of the road, the farmer met the second sly student, who, of course, had been waiting for him there.

"Where are you going with that sickly-looking goat?" the student asked.

193

"Hah!" laughed the farmer. "You students read books, but you're not very smart! Just a few minutes ago I met another of you, and he asked the same ridiculous question. Don't you know that this is a cow I'm taking to market, and not a goat?"

"My good man," said the student, "you have taken the wrong animal by mistake! May I suggest that the next time you want to sell a cow, you look at your animals more carefully, and *take* a cow."

And before the enraged farmer could say another word, the student courteously tipped his hat and continued on his way.

Just before the farmer reached the city gates, the third student approached him. "Good farmer," he said, "where are you going with that sad, scrawny goat?"

"Listen," cried the farmer, "I have already met two other students who have told me the same thing. But this is a cow, not a goat. At least I *think* it's a cow. Unless . . . unless . . . No, I'm sure it's a cow. It *is* a cow, isn't it? No? Oh dear! Maybe I did make an error, and mistakenly brought the goat instead of the cow."

"Well, we all make mistakes," the student consoled him. "But anyone who can see will tell you that the animal with you now is a goat. Undoubtedly your cow is still in your barn. But tell me, farmer, since you've come all this way, would you be interested in selling me the goat?"

"I might just as well sell it," thought the farmer, and turning to the student he asked how much the young man would pay.

The student generously offered to give him fifteen dollars. Said the farmer to himself, "That's a good price for a goat!" And he happily accepted the money.

When he returned home he told his wife that he had been lucky, and had received a good sum for their old goat.

"Did you say our *goat?*" questioned the wife. "You must be mistaken, dear husband. The goat is still in the barn. You took the cow to the market with you."

"I must be going mad!" shouted the farmer, and he rushed out of his house to the barn. There, sure enough, was the goat, peacefully chewing hay.

At last the farmer realized that the three students had made a fool of him. He dared not complain to the police or to the mayor, for then the whole town would soon be making fun of him. And so he thought and thought as he stood in the stall. And before long he smiled. "I'll get even with them," he said to himself. "More than even!"

That very same evening the farmer visited his best friend and borrowed a hundred and fifty dollars. Then he put on an old, well-worn cap, and walked into the city. When he reached an inn that was frequented by students, he called the innkeeper aside. "Here is fifty dollars," said the farmer. "The next time I come to this inn, serve me and my friends whatever we order. And when I ask for the bill, simply come over and tell us, *'It's already paid.'* Not a word more—do you understand?"

To this the innkeeper agreed, whereupon the farmer walked to two other inns and made similar arrangements.

Early the next morning the farmer dressed in his best Sunday suit, put on his shabby old cap and walked directly to the first inn. Upon arriving there, he ordered large quantities of food and fruits and delicious beverages.

Soon he saw his three pranksters enter the dining room. Cordially the farmer called them to this table, inviting them to sit with him and share a fine dinner. And since the farmer had pulled his little cap down over his forehead, and since he was dressed in his Sunday clothes, none of the students recognized him. Always eager to get something for nothing, the students sat down with him, and ordered the most expensive dishes on the menu.

When they had finished eating, the farmer asked the innkeeper for the bill. And as he did so, he took off his little cap and gave it a sudden twist. *"It's already paid,"* said the innkeeper.

The three students gasped with astonishment; the farmer, however, arose from the table, acting as if the innkeeper's answer were the most natural reply in the world. He bade the students farewell and returned home.

The next morning the farmer was up bright and early again. Once more he dressed in his Sunday suit, and once more he donned his old, worn cap.

Arriving at the city, he walked directly to the second inn. There too he waited only moments before the three students arrived; again, most cordially, he invited them to dine with him. Now he ordered the most elaborate meal the innkeeper could prepare; and when it was time to pay the bill, the farmer simply took off his little cap and gave it a sharp twist. The innkeeper walked to the table, smiled and said: *"It's already paid."* Without another word to the three students, the farmer arose and left.

"How does the farmer do it?" That question greatly occupied the minds of the students. For hour after hour they talked it over among themselves. They were quite sure that there was a definite relationship between the twisting of the cap and the mysterious payment of the bill. And so they finally concluded that the farmer's cap possessed some sort of magical power. Whereupon they decided that the next time they met the farmer they would try to buy his little cap.

The third day the farmer again walked to the city. At the third inn he again seemed surprised and delighted to see the students entering. Again he invited them to join him. And again all four ate a superb meal.

And again, of course, when it was time to pay the bill the farmer simply removed his little cap, gave it a sharp twist, and was promptly told by the innkeeper, *"It's already paid."*

But now when the farmer rose to leave, the three students begged him to sell them his cap.

"What, sell my cap?" the farmer replied indignantly. "Haven't you noticed how valuable it is? It is certainly worth much more than money because it pays for all my food bills, no matter how much I eat or drink."

This talk only served to make the students even more eager to possess the cap, and they offered the farmer five hundred dollars for it.

"You can't be serious," said the farmer. "Sell this marvelous cap for only five hundred dollars? You can't mean it! You must be joking!"

When they saw that he was about to leave, the students offered him seven hundred dollars, then eight hundred, and finally a thousand dollars.

"All right," the farmer said at last, "I know I shouldn't do this but then again I've had good use from the cap, and perhaps it ought now be somebody else's turn."

He took off the cap and looked at it sadly; but when the students handed him the thousand dollars, he put the money in his pocket and gave them the cap.

Arriving at home the farmer smiled at his wife, "I really don't understand students. First they buy my cow as a goat, and now they have bought my old worn cap for a thousand dollars. They certainly are a strange bunch."

And then he sat down in his easy chair, mightily pleased with the business he had conducted that week.

But the students?

They rushed off to the inn where they had first met the farmer. There they ordered a huge and sumptuous meal. When it was time to leave, the oldest of the three took the cap, gave it a sharp twist and then boldly asked the innkeeper for the bill. To his surprise the innkeeper came with pencil and paper in hand, did much careful calculating and handed him the bill. Frantically the student twisted the cap, but no matter how hard he twisted it and turned it, the anticipated words never crossed the innkeeper's lips. There was nothing the students could do but pay.

On the next day, the second student wore the hat, for he was convinced that his comrade hadn't twisted it properly. They went to the inn where they had dined with the farmer the second day, and here too they ordered a fine meal. When the time came to pay the bill, did the innkeeper say the magic words? No—he came with pen and paper. And again they had to pay.

On the third day the youngest student asserted that the other two just hadn't known how to use the cap. So they went to the third inn, where they ordered yet another elaborate repast. And when they had finished eating, the young student turned and twisted the cap so vigorously that it almost fell apart. Then he asked for the check. But to no avail! The landlord quickly added up the bill and gave it to the youngest student to pay.

When the students left the inn, they didn't know what to think. But they were most discouraged young men indeed.

Perhaps it took them another year of school training to learn that they had been tricked. Or perhaps they'll read it here for the first time!

The Wishing Ring

*Throughout the ages, man has accomplished great
things when he has had hope. This is aptly shown
in a fairy tale with a "twist" by the German
author, Richard Leander.*

From early morning until late, late at night, from the days v.hen he was a little child until now that he was a man, a farmer named Jon had labored in the fields. And never had he been able to grow all that he needed to feed his family or his cattle. Never did he have an extra penny. Never was he able to go to a fair or eat at the village inn. And never did he stop complaining.

One day, while he was in his field busily plowing and bitterly protesting his misfortunes, an old witch appeared at his side.

"Why do you work so hard when it doesn't get you anywhere?" she asked. Then she pointed a long, gnarled finger toward a hill on the horizon. "If you will merely walk in a straight line in that direction for two days, you will come to a pine tree that is taller than all the others surrounding it. And if you merely chop that tall tree down, your fortune will be made." The witch then disappeared as quietly and as quickly as she had come.

The farmer raised his axe to his shoulder and walked. And sure enough, after he walked for two full days, he found the pine tree. Immediately he set to work chopping it down. And when the tree began to sway, a bird's nest containing two eggs fell from the topmost branch. Then the tree smashed to the ground.

The earth trembled and the eggshells cracked open. From one hopped a fuzzy little eagle; from the other slipped a slender ring. The eagle grew instantly to a height of nine feet, flapped its wings and screeched, "You have freed me. I thank you. And as a reward, I give you the ring that fell from the other egg. Take good care of it, farmer, because it is no ordinary ring. It has the power to make one wish come true. But once that wish is fulfilled, the ring will then be no different

199

from any other ring. Therefore I warn you—before you speak your wish, consider carefully whether what you ask is what you really want. Otherwise you will regret it later on."

With that the eagle circled high into the sky. The farmer watched it until it disappeared from view. Then he slipped the ring on his finger and started for home. When he came to his town he went directly to the goldsmith, and asked what the ring was worth. The jeweler examined it. "Your ring is worth nothing," he said at last. "It's a plain old rusty iron band." When Jon heard this he laughed. "How little you know," he boasted. "This is really a *wishing* ring, and it's far more valuable than all the rings and gems you have in your shop."

The goldsmith was a greedy man, and now he saw an opportunity to get rich quickly. He invited the farmer to rest in his home and have dinner with him.

"No dinner, thank you. I must go home and tell my wife the news. But," he yawned, "I *am* tired, at that. I've walked for four full days without stopping. So if you don't mind, I will . . . stretch . . . out . . . and . . . take . . . a . . . little . . . nap." As soon as the farmer was safely snoring, the goldsmith gently took the wishing ring from Jon's finger, and replaced it with a similar but ordinary ring. And when the farmer awakened, he thanked the goldsmith for his hospitality, and continued on his way without knowing or even suspecting that he had been cheated.

But as soon as the goldsmith was alone, he rushed out of his home and ran to a cave in the hills. He blocked the entrance with a boulder so that no one could peek in or enter; and then he turned the ring and said, "I want to own one hundred thousand gold coins."

It started to rain gold inside the cave. Gold coins clinked to the ground—to the height of his ankles, then to the height of his knees, then to his fat belly, then as high as his chest. The jeweler couldn't move. And to his horror, the gold did not cease falling. A few minutes later he was buried under a ton of gold, in a cave that may never be found.

Meanwhile Jon arrived at his home, and showing the ring to his wife he said, "No longer are we going to lack anything. Our fortune is made. But we must think very carefully before we make our wish."

But his wife didn't have to think very long. She knew immediately what they needed. "We own so little land, dear Jon. Why don't we just ask for a few more acres?"

"No," he replied, "if I work hard for a year and have any

luck, we'll be able to buy the land. Our one wish must be saved for something very special."

And the farmer worked very hard and uncomplainingly for a year, and for the first time in his life he harvested a good crop. He then bought five more acres of land. "You see," he told his wife, "now we have the extra land, and we still have our wish."

The wife then suggested that he wish for some cattle. But again Jon replied that such a wish would be a wasted one, because with more hard work and some luck he would be able to buy the cattle the following year without using up the wish.

And so it happened. The farmer had an even better year, and was able to buy a whole new herd of cattle.

Then his wife said, "I really don't understand you, Jon. Before you owned the ring you always complained and wished for all sorts of things. But now you can have anything you desire—you could be a king, if you wished—yet you work harder than ever before, and are satisfied with everything. Why don't you make up your mind, and ask the magic ring."

"Wife, stop complaining!" replied the farmer. "We are still young and life is long. There is only one wish in the ring and that is easily used. Who knows what will still happen to us, and how useful that wish might be in the future?"

So one year followed the next. The farmer grew more and more successful, and the wish was still not wished.

Then, fifty happy years after the farmer had obtained the ring, he and his wife died on the same day. And the old farmer and his wife were buried with their magic ring—which actually wasn't a magic ring at all, and yet had somehow made their wishes come true.

It is a strange thing—how difficult it is, sometimes, to tell what is real and what is false. But this story does prove that a bad thing in good hands is much more valuable than a good thing in bad hands.

The Chief Astrologer

This folk tale about a man who was perhaps luckier than he deserved to be comes from Turkey, and probably dates from the 17th or 18th century.

In the largest city in Turkey, more years ago than the sky has stars, there once lived a cobbler, his wife, and their daughter. All morning long he cut leather for sandals and shoes. All afternoon he tacked and sewed and stitched. And at night he polished the shoes and decorated them.

One warm day, the cobbler's wife and daughter paid their weekly visit to the public baths. Just after they had filled the tub with warm, clear water, an attendant appeared. "Leave the room immediately," she ordered. "The wife of the chief astrologer has just arrived, and wants to use this tub."

So mother and daughter left that room and went to a second chamber, and again they carried buckets of water to a marble tub and filled it. Now another attendant arrived. "Leave at once," she too demanded. "The daughter of the chief astrologer is here, and wants to bathe in this tub." Disappointed, they tried a third room, only to learn that it was being used by the maids of the chief astrologer. Since no other rooms were available, there was nothing left for the two ladies to do but go home. How the cobbler's wife complained! And how jealous of the chief astrologer she grew! Because he was able to tell from the stars and from strange numbers what would happen in the future, he was second in power only to the sultan!

When the poor cobbler returned home from his shop that evening, he found his door locked. He knocked and rapped and called, but his wife would neither reply nor open the bolt. At last she raised the window and shouted, "Husband, before I let you into the house again, you must become chief astrologer."

"Dear wife," the old cobbler replied, "how can I possibly do that? I don't even know how to read or write."

"How you'll manage it is your problem," she snapped. "I only know that you must become chief astrologer, because that's the only way my daughter and I will ever be able to take a bath."

"Come, come," the perplexed man said. "Please be reasonable, dear wife."

"There's no sense arguing," the woman answered. "I won't let you in until you become chief astrologer, and that's all there is to it."

Well, the cobbler had been married to his wife for a long time, and he knew that once she made up her mind to something, nothing would change it. So he left the house and sadly walked back to town, sleeping most uncomfortably in a park. The next morning he shopped in the second-hand market and bought an old inkwell, a quill pen, and colorful old rags that he fashioned into a turban. Equipped in this manner he sat down at a street-corner and waited for someone who might want to have his fortune told.

Surprisingly enough, he didn't have to wait long. An old

gypsy walked up to him and said, "Greetings, astrologer, salaam. Do you really know how to tell fortunes and give magical advice? I have a terrible headache. I can't even sleep. When will it go? What can I do?"

The old cobbler knew absolutely nothing about medicine or cures for people. But he did know that some-times when he was ham-mering away at a shoe, and smacked his thumb instead of the tack with his hammer, it made him feel better if he hopped on one foot and then the other, shout-ing "Ow, poor thumb! Wow, poor thumb."

"Of course I can help you," he therefore an-swered. "Simply hop home, first on your left foot and then on your right. And when you hop on your left, shout 'Owperthum.' And when you hop on your right, shout 'Wowperthum.' And in the morning you'll be cured."

The gypsy paid him and did as she was told. She hopped all the way home, chanting, and when she got there she was so exhausted that she fell sound asleep immediately. And with one night of good sleep, her headache disappeared.

Very pleased indeed, the gypsy told her employer about this new astrologer, who knew his work so well that in a matter of minutes he had freed her from a headache that had plagued her for months.

"My, he does sound wonderful. Perhaps," the woman said, "he could cure my husband of his terrible temper."

"Certainly he can do that," the gypsy replied. "He's so good that he need not even see the master. I'm sure he can perform his magic if all I do is bring him the master's old red shirt."

"Take it," the woman said, "and also bring him this piece of gold. Tell him that if his cure works, I'll be happy to pay him more."

When the cobbler saw the old gypsy returning he was worried indeed. "She's back here to demand that I return her money," he thought to himself. "She's going to tell everyone that I'm a swindler."

But when he learned that the gypsy was apparently cured,

his confidence knew no limits. "Of course I can cure your master," he said. "But it will be difficult, so be silent while I think."

And then the old cobbler thought about his life at home. Whenever his wife or his daughter wanted something very much indeed —earrings, say, or a beautiful new veil—they put him into a good mood by cooking delectable breakfasts for him. Eggs with lamb and onions . . . his favorite dish! Or wheat and cucumber salad!

"Now," he said to the gypsy, "listen carefully. Give your mistress this shirt. Have her swing it around her head once on the first night, twice on the second, thrice on the third. Let her get up from her bed in the morning before the master arises, and swing it in the other direction. Once on the first day, twice on the second, thrice on the third. The first morning and the third morning she is to give him eggs for breakfast, with lamb and onions. And on the second day, wheat with cucumbers bought from a man with a black beard. And on the fourth day, he will be cured."

On the fifth day, the gypsy and her mistress rushed to the cobbler.

"You are a worker of miracles," they shouted. "He smiles as if he were the spring itself. He is as warm as the sun. As gentle as a breeze. We give you more gold with pleasure, most powerful astrologer."

Soon the cobbler's fame was so great that people had to stand in line to see him, and all paid him generously. But despite all these riches and success, his wife still didn't let him enter his own house because he wasn't yet the chief astrologer.

One day the sultan lost one of his most valuable and treasured rings. His castle was searched from parapets to underground storerooms—but no ring. Then one of the sultan's trusted advisers told him of a new astrologer who had performed a number of miracles. The sultan immediately commanded that this astrologer be brought before him.

The poor cobbler—for he it was—arrived. And the sultan ordered him to find the ring. "But" warned the sultan, "if you do not succeed, it will cost you your head."

The cobbler was sure that he was now near the end of his strange new career. How could he find the ring, when all the servants of the sultan had searched for it everywhere, for an entire week, and had not found it? But to gain a little time—and to enjoy himself briefly before certain death—he replied: "Your Excellency, it is not the custom of the stars to provide an immediate answer. Give me forty days, a room and good food. On the fortieth day I shall tell you where to find the ring."

The sultan agreed and the cobbler locked himself in his spacious and pleasant room. Every day he was served the delicious food of the court. And in order to keep track of the days, he kept one plate each day when servants came to his chamber to remove the dishes and goblets. After many days had passed, he decided to count the plates to see how many days were left before he had to confront the sultan. To his horror, only eighteen days remained. Angrily he said aloud: "Eighteen! Eighteen exactly, no more, no less."

Now it so happened that the thieves who had stolen the sultan's ring were actually servants of the sultan, and naturally they were concerned about everything that the astrologer did. As they were not permitted inside his room, they listened at his door. And when they heard him shout "Eighteen!" they shivered and paled with fear. Because "exactly eighteen, no more, no less" of the servants had participated in the theft. Now they were certain that the astrologer had discovered that eighteen people were guilty!

Hastily the thieves met and discussed the situation. Sure that the astrologer would next discover their identity, they decided to go to him first and confess their deed. Then they would beg for mercy, and perhaps he would be kind enough to save their lives.

Late that same evening, when everybody was asleep, the band of thieves unlocked the astrologer's door and entered his room. When the cobbler saw them he thought the sultan's men had come to fetch him. In despair he screamed, "Oh, it's you, is it?"

This frightened the thieves even more. Now they were convinced that the clever astrologer had already found them out. So they fell on their knees before him and wailed, "Yes, master, we are guilty. We took the ring, but have mercy on us for the sake of our wives and children. We swear to you by all that is holy that we will never steal again."

When the cobbler heard this, he quickly seized the opportunity offered him. With great dignity he lifted himself from his bed and walked among the men who were kneeling at his feet. "It is a lucky thing for you that you came to me just now. For I had just read your names in the stars."

"We don't doubt it, we don't doubt it," the thieves cried. "Have mercy on us, please have mercy."

"All right," the cobbler said, "I will forgive you, but you must do exactly as I say. On the fortieth day, feed the ring to one of the geese, and then clip the right wing of that goose, so that I can recognize her easily. Leave the rest up to me."

The thieves left the room muttering their thanks and praises, having promised to do his bidding.

On the fortieth day, the cobbler went before the sultan. "Well," said the ruler impatiently, "where is the ring?"

"Your Excellency," the cobbler replied calmly, "I have found the trace of your ring and I expect to find the ring itself today. But first you must command all the people in your castle to pass before me."

The sultan gave the order and soon everybody—beginning with the most exalted ministers of state down to the poorest dishwashers —passed before the astrologer. And when the thieves passed by him, the astrologer just smiled at them, but didn't say a word. Then he said to the sultan, "Your Excellency, there are no thieves among your staff. Now, order that all your animals be brought before me, because I have read in the stars that your ring is in the castle, and it is kept by some-one or something that is alive."

The sultan again gave the command, and this time a long procession of camels, oxen and cows, horses, lambs, and goats and finally chickens and geese paraded before him. And at the very end of this long line waddled a goose with its right wing clipped. The astrologer seized the animal and ordered that its stomach be opened. And to the amazement of all, the ring was found.

The sultan was overjoyed and promptly appointed the old cobbler the chief astrologer of his court.

That evening when the cobbler returned home he was at last admitted.

And the next morning when his wife and daughter went to the bathhouse they were greeted with the honors due the family of a high dignitary in the sultan's court.

And when she returned home clean and satisfied, she turned to her husband and said, "Now, husband, you can go back to your old profession because you are no more an astrologer than I am a bird, and when the sultan discovers this he will chop off your head."

But the cobbler shook his head and said, "My dear wife, I can't just walk out on my job. The sultan wouldn't like that at all."

"That, husband," the woman replied, "is your problem."

The next day the cobbler returned to the court and told the sultan that he wanted to leave his post. But the sultan wouldn't hear of it. "You want to leave because you do not earn enough," said the sultan. "And so I hereby double your salary."

Each day of the following week, the cobbler's wife said, "Well, husband, I'm losing patience. You'd better find some way to be a cobbler again!" But the poor man could think of nothing. Then one day she finally declared, "Well, husband, my daughter and I are going to the public bath this afternoon. And if you're still chief astrologer when we return, you'll not come in this house again."

Dejected and perplexed, the cobbler made his way to the palace. And as he walked, suddenly a procession came by. It was the sultan —on his way to the public bath.

"No!" screamed the cobbler. "NO—THE SULTAN MUST NOT GO TO THE BATH!"

For if he does, the cobbler reasoned, *my wife and daughter will lose their rooms and tubs. And then my wife will never rest until I become sultan of all the land!*

The sultan's advisers had heard the cobbler's shout, and they rushed to their ruler's side.

"Your chief astrologer forbids it," they told him. "We heard him scream that you must not go to the baths!"

And so the sultan turned back. How fortunate that he did so —for in moments a terrible storm arose, and lightning struck the baths, destroying them completely. The cobbler's wife and daughter were nearing the baths when this happened. They turned and ran, and didn't stop running until they reached home.

Meanwhile the sultan tearfully and thankfully embraced the cobbler. He tripled his salary and told him that anything he wished for would be his for the asking.

To the sultan's great disappointment the cobbler asked only that he be permitted to give up his position as head astrologer. And because the sultan always kept his word, he gave the cobbler a cart filled with gold pieces, and permitted him to leave.

Immediately he returned home and became a cobbler once more. And as his wife made no further demands on him, he lived happily with her and his daughter for many, many years.

The Clever Thief

The arrogant, rich man who gets his just desserts is a popular folklore theme throughout the world. This version is from Greece. The author is unknown.

You must never, never laugh at the mistakes or misfortunes of others. Let me tell you about a man who did.

He was a wealthy man, and boastful; and one day, while sitting at a table in a coffee shop, he chanced to overhear a conversation that greatly interested him. Two merchants at the next table were complaining bitterly about thefts that had recently taken place in their homes. The rich man had never been robbed.

"I've never been robbed," he said to his two neighbors. "And if you two have been the victims of thieves, it was entirely your own fault that the robberies took place. If you had not been so careless with your valuables, they would never have been stolen. And so," he concluded smugly, "it seems to me that you got just what you deserved. Perhaps it will teach you a lesson. I *know* that such a thing could never happen in my house."

What the rich man did not know, however, was that a thief was sitting near them, and was also listening with considerable interest. *Now you just wait*, the thief thought to himself. *I'm going to teach you a lesson you'll remember as long as you live!*

Spying the rich man's pipe on the table, the thief snatched it and quietly walked out of the coffee shop. He went directly to the rich man's home, and knocked on the door. When the rich man's wife opened the door, the thief politely said, "The master has sent me with a message. You are to give me two copper pots, because he wants to buy butter and honey at the market."

"How do I know you are telling the truth?" the wife asked suspiciously.

The thief pulled the stolen pipe from his pocket, and answered, "He gave me his pipe to show to you."

When the woman saw her husband's pipe, she believed the thief's story, and handed him two large copper pots. He sped to the market, had one filled with butter and the other with honey, and then carried them back to the woman.

About fifteen minutes later he once more returned to the rich man's home. He knocked on the door, showed the pipe again, and said, "Now the master needs a thousand gold pieces, because he wants to purchase gifts for you at the goldsmith's."

Since there was no reason for the woman to doubt the word of this quick and courteous messenger, she handed him a large bag of gold pieces. "Now I must take them to the master," said the thief, and he departed.

Meanwhile the husband was about ready to leave the coffee shop. When he couldn't find his pipe, he decided to go home at once, thinking that his wife would know where he had put it. When he asked her, she laughed.

"My, my, you *are* absent-minded today!" she replied. "Don't you remember that you gave your pipe to the man you sent here first for the two copper pots and then for the thousand gold pieces?"

"Thousand gold pieces?" exclaimed her husband. He leaped from his seat and rushed out the door. "Thief, thief," he screamed, "I've been robbed!" And he ran through the city, searching for the thief.

Scarcely had the rich man passed through his own gate, than the thief—who had been concealing himself in the bushes—returned to the house. He thrust his arm through an open window and cried: "Good woman, quickly give me your husband's golden sword. He has caught the thief."

The wife was so happy to hear this message that without a second thought she passed her husband's golden sword through the window.

Now the thief owned a pipe, a valuable golden sword, and a thousand gold coins. Content at last he left the city, never to be seen again.

A few hours later the husband hobbled home, footsore and tired and hungry, dismayed by his failure to capture the thief.

"Well, my dear husband," his wife greeted him. "I am so glad you caught the thief. Did you manage to get all our money back?"

"I never caught the thief," the man grumbled. "What makes you think I did?"

"But you sent a messenger to me for your golden sword as soon as you caught the thief!"

Now the rich man's bellows of rage almost shattered the windows. Again he scrambled from his seat and ran into the streets to search for the robber. But his quest was in vain, and soon the unhappy man realized that the thief had indeed escaped.

As he limped home he recalled how foolishly he had sneered and boasted at the coffee shop. And the rich man vowed that in the future he would never again laugh at anyone's misfortunes.

A good vow for us all!